# Babies
## for Beginners

Roni Jay

# Babies
## for Beginners

Keeping your baby happy and healthy

white
**LADDER**

This edition first published in Great Britain 2009 by
Crimson Publishing, a division of Crimson Business Ltd
Westminster House
Kew Road
Richmond
Surrey
TW9 2ND

ISBN 978 1 90541 044 6

Typeset by Julie Martin Ltd
Printed and bound by Legoprint SpA, Trento

# Acknowledgements

I would like to thank Rich for teaching me everything I needed to know when our first baby was born (and then doing half of it himself). I would also like to express my deepest gratitude to Jack, Ned and Hal who afforded me the chance to practise it – especially the being up all night bit which thanks to them I got really good at (although never entirely enthusiastic about).

I would also like to thank Dr Sally Roberts and Carol Westwood for checking the manuscript for me with a thoroughly professional eye, and Dr Ginny Cunliffe for her help with this new edition. Thanks also to Eleanor Turner for her help with the third edition.

# Contents

Introduction                                        1

1   Giving birth to the baby                        5
2   Holding the baby                               21
3   Breast versus bottle                           27
4   Breastfeeding                                  37
5   Bottle feeding                                 49
6   Tackling wind                                  57
7   Sterilising                                    63
8   Changing the nappy                             69
9   Tackling nappy rash                            79
10  Bathtime                                       85
11  Dressing the baby                              91
12  Stopping the baby crying                       99
13  Where to put the baby to sleep                107
14  Getting the baby to go to sleep              117
15  Taking the baby for a walk                    131
16  Taking the baby in the car                    137
17  Playing with the baby                         143
18  Weaning onto solid food                       151
19  Teething                                      163
20  Travelling with the baby                      169

Appendix
    Things not to worry about                     179
    Things to consider worrying about             187
    Basic equipment                               192

A final word...                                   195

# Disclaimer

*Babies for Beginners* has been read, checked and approved by Dr Sally Roberts, a family GP, and Carolyn Westwood, a midwife and health visitor. Both are also mothers.

However, neither the publisher, the author, nor these professionals, can accept any responsibility for the material in this book. It is intended as advice and help, not as medical instruction.

The advice in *Babies for Beginners* assumes that your baby is normal and healthy; any illness or disability may require certain kinds of care which overrule anything contained in this book.

I'd also like to add that babies don't come with guarantees. There's always one that doesn't sleep any better on formula milk than on breast milk, or which hates being rocked. All the information in here goes for the vast majority of babies, but I can't promise that yours will conform in every way.

If you have any concerns about your own baby you should consult your GP, health visitor or midwife. Or your mother, of course, who will doubtless be full of useful suggestions.

# Introduction

There are plenty of activities in life that seem daunting when you first try them, even though you will feel confident and expert within a few weeks or months: your first job, driving a car, learning to swim, long division (OK, fair enough, you may never feel comfortable with that one). Of all the activities that quickly become second nature, however, being a parent has to be the most daunting in the initial stages.

The results of failure seem inconceivably dreadful. Suddenly you're responsible for this tiny, fragile and infinitely precious thing, and you don't feel up to the job. Who decided you were fit to be left in charge?

In fact, we all feel like this about our first baby, and it lasts only a few weeks. You get the occasional brief recurrence when you encounter a major new issue such as solid food, or teething, but in the main the beginner stage lasts only for a month or two.

This book is designed to get you through those first few weeks, and answer all those questions you don't yet know you have.

For example, you'll find a few books out there which tell you what 'wind' is and how to wind a baby but, as a new parent, your first question on winding is, 'How will I know when it needs winding?'

This modest volume is the beginner's bible. If it isn't in here, you don't need to know it. I haven't bothered with all the extra stuff, the fancy equipment, the icing on the cake bits of first time parenthood. Save that for the next baby. First time round you need to build your confidence, not be undermined by reminders about all the things you could be doing but aren't.

Because the truth is that most of it is unnecessary. Three quarters of the equipment in baby shops is surplus to requirements. It might make your life easier – and by all means buy it if you can afford it – but it won't make you a better parent.

If the baby is warm, comfortable, well fed and able to sleep when it needs to, you're doing a great job. Save all the rest for when you've mastered these basics.

I'm often frustrated by how insecure many first time parents are about their abilities, when in fact they're clearly doing a good job. Looking after a baby isn't as hard as the modern baby industry, and all those well meaning friends and relatives, might make it appear. People have been doing it successfully for tens of thousands of years. So as long as your baby is happy and healthy, and you don't keep dropping it, don't let anyone tell you you're not doing it right.

A lot of the trick to mastering parenthood is about keeping your focus firmly on what really matters. In this book I've specified, for each activity, the core objective and the key focus. So if you're bathing the baby the core objective is to get the baby cleaner than it was when you started, but the key focus is not to drown it. If the baby comes out of the bath not drowned, you're a good parent. If it's also cleaner than it started – even only a little bit – you're earning bonus brownie points.

Keeping your focus clearly on the essentials – not dropping, drowning, freezing or starving the baby – is all it takes to be a decent parent at this stage. So don't knock yourself. All the rest will slot into place within weeks and you'll graduate from beginner to expert before you know it.

I've used the word 'it' to describe your baby throughout this book. There are several reasons for this:

- I don't know if your baby is a boy or a girl.

- You quite possibly don't know either if you're reading this before the birth (which I'd advise).

Before your baby is born, and in the first few weeks, the baby often feels like an object as much as a person.

This may be even truer for fathers than for mothers. It's easy to feel that this object has arrived without instructions, and you're floundering around trying to work out how to operate it. The beginner stage really lasts from when this object turns up through to when it feels fully like your child and a real personality in its own right. When you reach this point, you won't be a beginner any more.

I hope that this book will not only tell you everything you need to know to keep your baby happy and healthy through the first weeks and beyond, but will also give you the confidence to enjoy the experience, and to be able to tell anyone who criticises you to sod off.

# Giving birth

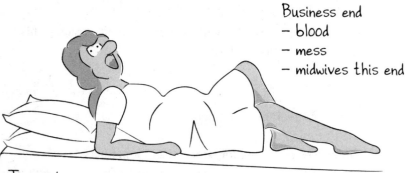

Business end
– blood
– mess
– midwives this end

Top end
– noise
– abuse
– heavy breathing
– father should stay this end

# 1

# Giving birth to the baby

If you want to be a parent, sooner or later that baby is going to have to come out. In fact, even if you didn't want to be a parent, it would still have to come out. During pregnancy, a huge amount of focus is on the relatively brief process of transferring the baby from inside the body to outside the body.

**Core objective:** Get the baby out

**Key focus:** Stay as relaxed as you can

Mothers (and indeed fathers) quite understandably worry about labour and birth. This is true of every baby, but especially the first one. You've no idea what to expect. What's more, there's no shortage of people ready to tell you horror stories about their labour, or the awful things that happened during their sister's husband's best friend's girlfriend's labour.

Of course you're nervous. But that doesn't mean it won't all be fine. The anticipation can be far worse than the event.

---

## Myth: labour is always long and excruciatingly painful

There's no denying that, unfortunately, this is sometimes the case. But many labours are relatively short and, while I've never heard of an entirely painless labour (except under anaesthetic), many mothers report that the pain is perfectly bearable.

---

# GETTING IT IN PERSPECTIVE

Take what other people tell you with a pinch of salt. Their labour may have been horrendous according to their accounts, but lots of people's aren't. Remember too that it makes a far better story if they make it sound really gory and unpleasant, and, while they're not lying to you, they may be embellishing for effect. Think about all those people you know who haven't told you about their dreadful labours – that's because they didn't have dreadful labours.

Many midwives report that they can predict with considerable accuracy how a labour will go as soon as the mother arrives in the delivery ward. If the mother is terrified and demanding that they start preparing the strongest possible painkillers right now, they know the labour will go badly. If, on the other hand, the mother turns up with a smile and a sense of adventure – albeit a little apprehensive – the labour is almost always easy (bar the unlucky few).

The important thing to focus on is the fact that the ultimate aim is to get the baby out and for it to be healthy.

We all know the occasional sad case of a baby that didn't make it out healthy, but think about how many more people you know who – for all their troubles on the way – produced babies which were perfectly fine. You probably know of one or two labours that went seriously wrong, compared with many hundreds or more which ultimately achieved their goal – a healthy mother and baby.

# THE PROCESS (FOR THE MOTHER)

This isn't a medical guide to giving birth, just a few pointers to help you. The most important thing to bear in mind is that even if you do nothing, the baby will still come out and you can't stop it.

Anything you do to help either the process or yourself is a bonus. You can't get giving birth wrong.

I should add that these guidelines assume that there are no significant complications, which is the case for the majority of births. If complications do arise, obviously you should listen to the advice of the medical professionals around you.

1  **Recognise that you're in labour.** Your waters may or may not break before the contractions begin; in fact they may not break until the baby starts to appear (although this is unusual). But however it starts, being in labour is a bit like being in love – you'll know it when it happens. If you're not certain, it may be the start of labour but you still don't need to do anything about it until you're sure.

2  **Get yourself where you want to be.** At hospital, at home, wherever you've planned. Round up your partner or whoever is attending the birth, and your hospital bag, and head for where you want the baby to be born. Unless the contractions are within about three minutes of each other you don't need to panic about this.

Stay as relaxed as you can. If you're out and can't get at your hospital bag, don't worry about it. There's nothing in there that can't wait until someone has the chance to collect it for you later.

3  **Remember anything you've learnt about breathing exercises and so on.** Start practising now before the contractions get stronger and closer together, and it will make it much easier to remember them later on.

4  **Do whatever you feel like doing.** Hell, you can even get away with swearing at complete strangers who are trying to help you. This is the best chance you'll ever get to be selfish,

so milk it. If you want to walk around, walk around. If you want to sit in a wheelchair and spin round in circles, demand a wheelchair. It's your labour – so do it your way.

5   **Painkillers are your choice.** At my first labour, one midwife told me I couldn't be in labour because I wasn't asking for painkillers (I gave birth three hours later). You may want painkillers from the start, or not until the end, or not at all.

Don't let anyone else tell you what pain you can and can't stand.

6   **Tell the midwives when you want to push.** You'll know when you're ready to push, believe me. It's an almost irresistible urge. Once you tell the midwife you've reached this point, she'll give you your instructions.

7   **Focus on the end product.** If the pain – or even just the frequency of it – becomes intense towards the end, keep telling yourself that in a few minutes you'll meet the baby face-to-face for the first time. As you near the actual birth, just focus on the baby and do whatever the midwives tell you. Pain or not, this stage should also be very exciting and that will get you through.

8   **Give birth.** This bit's easy. It happens pretty quickly and whether you like it or not. And as soon as you do it, the pain stops. OK, there's still discomfort, but you notch down to about two per cent of the previous level, and boy does it feel good. More important still, you get to meet the baby at last.

## Caesarean section

If you have to have an emergency caesarean, you may be under general anaesthetic in which case you won't need any instructions from me. However if you have an elective C-section, or an emergency one under local anaesthetic, here's what will happen.

1 Your partner should be allowed to be with you throughout the process (whatever they may tell you to the contrary).

2 A needle will be inserted into your lower back to give you the epidural or spinal block to numb the bottom half of your body.

3 You will also have a catheter to drain your bladder, and a drip in your hand or arm for administering extra fluids, pain killers and so on. And you may also have a heart monitor.

4 The medical team will put up a screen so you and your partner don't have to watch the gory bits, however the doctor should give you a running commentary.

5 The doctor will make two incisions and then the baby can be lifted out. This won't take more than a few minutes. Once the baby is out and checked over it will be handed to you (unless there are complications and it needs to be taken straight to the special care baby unit). You can hold it during the rest of the procedure.

6 The doctor will spend about half an hour delivering the placenta and then stitching you up, closing each layer of muscle or skin in turn.

You will be uncomfortable after the birth (no surprises there) as you have had major surgery. However you'll be encouraged to get out of bed after a few hours and should be home in a few days.

If you've had significant surgery of any kind in the past you'll have some clue as to how this will feel. However last time you may not have had a newborn baby to deal with at the same time. Any help you can line up will probably be a good thing.

## What sort of pain should you expect?

It takes, very roughly speaking, a certain number of contractions to get the baby out. This means that if the labour is very long, at least you won't have to put up with very frequent contractions for most of it. Exhaustion, after the first missed night's sleep, will be the worst of it. If the contractions are close together, on the other hand, it's harder work but it won't last nearly so long. A few hours at most probably, if the contractions start off only a few minutes apart. So you might get long and tiring, or you might get really hard work. But – although nothing is guaranteed – you're very unlikely to get both.

Regardless of the timescale, however, here's an idea of what you can expect in terms of pain. It's impossible to describe pain precisely, and not every woman feels the pain of labour in exactly the same way. But here's the best description I can give you.

● Contractions feel pretty similar to the cramps you get during your period. They start relatively far apart and get closer together as the labour progresses. Equally, they start off pretty mild, and become stronger. And they last longer as they go on. So you go from what feels like fairly normal period pains to something which feels the same but much stronger and longer (usually about 90 seconds from start to finish eventually).

Between contractions, there is generally no pain whatsoever. This means that although I can't pretend that those people who describe labour as painful are lying to you, the pain isn't constant.

- You may get backache in your lower back during contractions; this is very common. In fact, I can honestly say that I personally found the backache more painful than the contractions during my first labour. Backache is exacerbated by constipation, so eat plenty of bran cereals for the last couple of weeks of pregnancy and you've a far better chance of avoiding it.

- Generally speaking, movement helps ease (or at least distract from) the pain, as well as speeding up labour. So rather than lie on a bed, you'll be better off walking around or keeping mobile generally. If the labour looks like it will be going on for a while, you'll need to balance this with the issue of exhaustion. Even if you're only shuffling around the delivery ward, after a few hours of labour you could notch up quite a respectable mileage. So rest between contractions, and move through them.

- The second stage of labour, as it's known, is the bit where you start pushing to get the baby out. Look, I don't want to be crude here, but pushing a baby out really doesn't feel that different to pushing out other things that you've pushed out before from that region of your anatomy. Yep, giving birth feels pretty much like going to the loo after the most serious bout of constipation you can imagine. In fact, if you have been constipated lately, you'll be doing that too – the baby can't get out if the bowel is blocked and, since the baby won't stay put, the bowel simply has to empty. This will happen during the second stage if you haven't managed to shift it sooner. Contemplating this in advance you might think that it would be deeply embarrassing. All I can say is that by this stage in labour, when you finally get there, all your embarrassment sensors have become blocked, and it's really no big deal. Also, the midwives deal with it every day and honestly don't care. Their totally matter-of-fact approach to it will make it impossible to feel very embarrassed.

- By the end of the second stage, everything is pretty intense. Contractions are close together and more painful (although many women find the second stage less painful than the first), and the midwives will be calmly issuing instructions ('breathe', 'don't push for a minute', and that sort of thing – echoed by your partner who hasn't a clue what else to say but figures if the midwives are saying it, it must be right).

The whole second stage may last only a matter of minutes and this last, most intense part, could well go on for only two or three minutes.

- If you need a forceps delivery to help the baby out, this can be uncomfortable and you'll be offered some kind of pain relief if you don't already have an epidural or other form or pain killer. Ventouse (suction cup) assisted delivery shouldn't need additional pain relief.

- You will have heard that many women tear when they give birth. Although a good midwife can reduce this (by advising you not to push until you've had time to stretch a bit more) it may still happen. The important thing to know is that you probably won't even feel it. So don't fret about it – there's so much going on, and you're so spaced out by this time, that it won't figure at all.

- That's right – spaced out. The good news about labour is that your body goes into overdrive producing hormones to help you cope with the process of getting the baby out. Within a few short hours of labour beginning you'll start to feel slightly spaced out, or woozy, to the point that if you're tired you may actually drift off between contractions even if they are only three or four minutes apart. By the end of the labour, these hormones have got you to a state where the whole experience takes on a dreamlike quality, you have absolutely no sense of time and, if it weren't for the contractions, you'd be having the best trip of your life (and it's legal). If you've chosen to use gas and air or pethidine these may make you feel lightheaded or woozy too.

- Once the baby is born, the pain level plummets to a point which, compared with what has gone before, seems entirely bearable. The third stage of labour – where you give birth to the placenta – is very quick and should feel uncomfortable but no worse.

After the birth, your body may go into shock briefly. In other words, you may feel very cold and start to shiver uncontrollably. The midwives are used to this and will have you warmed up and comfortable very quickly.

- You will continue to feel uncomfortable, especially when you move around, for several days. Most of the lower part of your body will feel badly bruised. However, you should be able to get perfectly comfortable in bed, and be able to get to the bathroom (and to the baby, of course). As with bruising, your recovery will be on a steady upward trend and within a day or two you'll feel well enough to move around far more.

# THE PROCESS (FOR THE FATHER)

As an involved and supportive father-to-be, you'll want to be as helpful as possible at the birth. But what on earth are you supposed to do? You've never done this before, and suddenly you're going to be in the thick of things. Well, the following guidelines should help.

- Treat your partner as if she's the boss and you're her willing servant throughout labour. Just do as she says. It's only a few hours, after all, and she really is doing the toughest job so it's not unreasonable to ask you to do everything else.

- When your partner tells you she's in labour, don't panic. Just say something along the lines of, 'Are you, darling? That's nice. What would you like me to do?' And then drop everything. Don't say, 'Man United have just equalised and there's only 20 minutes to go. Can't you just hang on before I run you to the hospital?'

Parenthood is all about sacrifice, and this is where it starts.

- Equally, if she goes into labour during the night (which is extremely common), don't make a fuss about being woken up.

Be as calm and reassuring as you can. Obviously this comes more naturally to some than to others, but she knows you and she won't expect more than your best effort.

- Try to remember the things which will be important to her. She'll be very impressed by comments such as, 'I'll just put your hospital bag in the car while you nip to the loo.'

- Drive carefully on the way to the hospital, and avoid any bumps and potholes. If you can't avoid them, apologise anyway (I know you didn't put them there but this is no time to get picky).

- Don't drive too fast. Recognise that no matter how fast you drive, it won't be fast enough, so you might as well have her scream at you to hurry at 40mph as at 80mph.

- By the time you get to the delivery ward, you may have started to feel more confident and in control. However, the sight of the midwives – who really do know what they're doing – will instantly make you feel like a spare part again. Do what they tell you; they know best.

- Having said that, just occasionally you will encounter someone who tries to pressurise you into doing something you don't want. This is where you come into your own. Your partner will not have her usual strength and assertiveness, and may need you to stick up for her if the need arises. If, for example, she asks for pain relief and the midwife says to wait, it's your job to be firm and insist that what your partner wants, your partner gets. Now.

If the labour is slow, the midwife may try to send you away for a few hours. If this is not what your partner wants, be firm and refuse to go.

However, it's not helpful to fall out badly with the midwives, so stay polite and pleasant despite your firm insistence.

- Stay out of the midwives' way. Your place is with your partner, so just hold her hand and you can't get into mischief.

- If you've been to antenatal classes, and paid attention, you'll know when your partner should be breathing fast or deep or whatever. So remind her.

If she screams, 'I'm not a bloody idiot! I know how to breathe!' don't take this personally. (But do stop reminding her, at least for a while.)

- Your partner will be experiencing many deep emotions and a great deal of pain. If her way of dealing with this involves hurling abuse at her nearest and dearest, feel flattered that this means you. On no account take offence, or hold her in any way responsible for anything she says during labour. She is likely to blame you for getting her into this condition in the first place, threaten never to have sex with you again etc etc. This is par for the course. However unpalatable you find this aspect of labour, just remember that she's still the one who has drawn the short straw.

- There will be blood, and lots of it. Sorry if this bothers you but it's best to find out now. It should all be 'healthy' blood, and doesn't signify that anything is wrong. Just don't wear your best clothes. Your safest bet is to stay up the other end of the proceedings and talk to your partner.

- What should you say to her? This isn't really a situation you feel life has prepared you for, and you may be unclear about how to make conversation with your partner under these conditions. She may well, for much of the time, behave quite normally of course, and chat away happily. At other times, and especially during the later stages, you may not get much response from her. This doesn't mean she won't appreciate you talking to her. Here are some suggestions:

  o Tell her how well she's doing

  o Reassure her that it won't be long now

  o Remind her about her breathing (if you dare)

  o Pass on any instructions from the midwife

- You can repeat anything you say several times, as she may be withdrawing into a trance-like state and repetition will help to get through to her. If you make eye contact with her this will help her to hear you, and will prevent you looking at what's going on down the other end.

Your role here is important; the midwives are primarily interested in your partner's, and the baby's, physical health. You are responsible for offering her mental and emotional support.

Oh, and a word about humour: it can be very helpful, but only if you're entirely certain of her response. Don't push it – a sense of humour can be the first casualty of labour.

- When the baby is born, it will be covered in blood and slime. Your job will be to react - instantly and honestly - with a completely positive approach. Tell your partner how clever she is (even though we all know that stupid people give birth too), and how beautiful the baby is.

- You may be itching to hold the baby - after all it is yours as much as hers - but I'm afraid you have to give her first refusal on this. The chances are she'll hand it over to you pretty soon while she gets sorted out, cleaned up and into bed - and at least by then a lot of the blood will have smeared off onto her, so it's no bad thing really.

At the end of all this, you may wonder what bloody use you were. But the chances are that your partner will feel – whether she admits it or not – hugely reassured that you were there.

# Supporting the baby

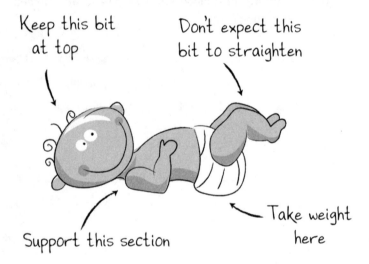

Keep this bit
at top

Don't expect this
bit to straighten

Support this section

Take weight
here

# Holding the baby

Once your baby has been born, you'll find that you can't operate it fully unless you hold it from time to time. In fact, you may find yourself overcome by a strange desire to hold it for no real reason at all. But is there a right way and a wrong way to hold a baby?

**Core objective:** Hold the baby using nothing but your arms to support it

**Key focus:** Don't injure it

---

## Myth: if you don't hold your baby exactly right, it will suffer sever injuries

Actually, there are lots of right ways to hold a baby, and only one or two wrong ones. What's more, most of the wrong ones are pretty obvious, such as upside down by one toe (no need to check this to see if I'm right).

---

# THE PROCESS

1 **Prepare yourself.** Until you're really au fait with picking a baby up, you need consciously to make sure you're ready before you begin. For example, put down anything else you're carrying to make more room in your arms for the baby. And stand in a stable posture; don't reach out for the baby from a distance while precariously balanced on one leg.

2 **Support the baby's head.** No doubt you'll have heard this before. (What may not have been made so clear is that this is pretty well the only rule.) Due to some design flaw of nature, a baby can't actually hold the weight of its own head. While it's lying down this isn't really a problem, but once you start to lift it from the ground (or wherever you normally keep it), you can see that its head will tend to stay where it is while the rest of its body moves upwards. At best, this makes it quite hard for the baby to breathe. If you lift it up really quickly, you can cause whiplash injuries. The obvious piece of equipment for supporting the baby's head is your hand, so slide it carefully under the baby's head.

3   **Lift the baby.** Fortunately, you have another hand. This is just what you need to complete the lifting process. Since babies are inherently very light, this second hand is all you should need to lift the baby up. Approach the baby with this hand from the other side. Make sure you have a firm grip before you begin. Best to move gently – it's a baby, after all, not a handbag or a rugby ball. Remember to keep your two hands moving at vaguely the same speed, so that the baby's head (in one hand) and its body (in the other) can maintain a roughly constant distance from each other.

It doesn't matter which way the baby is facing relative to your body, or whether it is vertical or horizontal, so long as if it's vertical, its head is uppermost.

4   **Hold the baby.** The reason people often hold babies in that traditional manner lying along the adult's arm, head nestled into the armpit, is because it's easy – not because it's the only way. It means the baby's head is supported by your upper arm, its body by your lower arm and hand, and look: you've got a whole free arm left over. Handy. There are lots of other ways to hold a baby, however – just keep its head supported and higher than its feet. You can have it face up or face down; it probably won't mind and it may indicate a preference (this is usually clear by whether it yells or not when you change position).

5   **Put it down.** When you've finished holding the baby, you can put it down again. Essentially you need to reverse the picking up process. Decide where you are going to put it down before you begin, or you may encounter difficulties in an otherwise straightforward procedure. Now lower the baby – at any angle but with its head supported – until it comes to rest on the

surface you have selected. Don't remove your hands until the baby's weight has transferred to the new surface otherwise you will, in effect, drop it.

# ADVANCED BABY HOLDING

1 **Moving about.** As time goes on, you'll want to hold the baby while moving about, or even doing other things at the same time. The key rules here are:

   ○ Wear sensible shoes

   ○ Look where you're going.

If you feel ready to start doing things while you're holding the baby, this is where a holding position which leaves a whole arm free really earns its keep.

If you're right-handed, you'll probably find it easiest to hold the baby in your left arm and leave your right hand free. If you're left-handed you'll find the reverse most comfortable. Either way, you can impress your friends with how naturally you've taken to parenthood, as you skilfully sterilise bottles, wash baby clothes or tidy the kitchen while balancing a baby on one arm.

2 **Using a sling.** A baby sling is somewhere to put your baby while you get on with things. Instead of leaving it yelling on the other side of the room, you put the baby in the sling, which is attached to yourself so the baby is right there. This tends to quieten it down, so it's especially useful if you're making phone calls or holding conversations. Also on a positive note, the baby will be happier. Don't try to insert the baby before

you have the sling fastened to your body, or the baby may drop straight through it. Follow the instructions that come with the sling properly.

3 **Put the baby on your hip.** This is purely optional. But once the baby is about three months, and can support its own head, you can sit it on your hip while you move around. It will not, however, balance there on its own. You will need to put an arm round its back with your hand under its bottom.

# Breast versus bottle

Even before your baby is born, you'll be deluged with advice about how to get milk into it. The breastfeeding/bottle feeding debate can get very heated, and until you've tried at least one of the options you may not feel confident about which side of the debate you're on.

**Core objective:** Get milk into the baby

**Key focus:** Have a healthy, happy baby

You may have strong views about how you want to feed your baby when it's born, or you may not. Either way, the important thing to remember is that how you feed it is entirely your choice, and no one else's business. There isn't a right way.

---

## Myth: if you don't breastfeed your baby you're a bad parent

You can't tell looking at a child or even an adult whether they were breast or bottle fed. It doesn't show in their looks, their personality or their health, so how can it possibly be that important? Answer: it can't.

---

# THE DIFFERENCES

There are several aspects of looking after your baby where you will notice a difference between breast and bottle feeding, so I'll just run through the key ones and you can think about which version suits you.

## The baby

Babies are not, frankly, connoisseurs. They will drink whatever kind of milk you put in front of them. If you give them a choice of breast or bottled milk, they won't generally express a preference on the taste front. However, there are one or two other points to consider:

| Breast | Bottle |
|---|---|
| The baby will need to spend more time feeding since breast milk is less filling. | The baby will be able to spend less time feeding – and maybe more sleeping – if you bottle feed it. |
| Breast milk is perfectly designed over millions of years of evolution to give your baby exactly the nutrients and hormones that it needs, and to help the baby's immunity. | Formula milk (that's the technical term for what goes in the bottle) lacks some human hormones and the like which are in breast milk, but it contains all the essential nutrients and has nothing harmful in it. |
| The baby will enjoy the physical closeness of breastfeeding. | Father and baby get more chance to bond as he can take his turn bottle feeding. |

## The practicalities

We'll go into the practical details of breast and bottle feeding in the next couple of chapters. But it's worth looking at one or two comparisons:

| Breast | Bottle |
|---|---|
| You can breastfeed a baby one-handed, leaving your other hand free for other tasks, such as holding a cold drink. | One hand for the baby, one hand for the bottle. For the vast majority of parents, this is the full quota of hands used up. |
| If your baby is in your bedroom with you, you don't have to get out of bed to feed it in the night. | Unless you equip yourself with an array of bottle warming equipment etc, you have to get up in the night (while your baby yells) to sort out and warm the bottle. |

| Breast | Bottle |
|---|---|
| Only the baby's mother can breastfeed the baby. | Anyone who knows what they're doing can bottle feed the baby – either parent, a visiting midwife, or anyone else who unwittingly calls round at feeding time. |
| You don't have to spend time sterilising, cleaning and filling bottles. | There's quite a lot of gear that goes with bottle feeding, and you need to spend time cleaning and sterilising. If you travel, all this stuff has to go with you. |
| You can feed your baby pretty much instantly when it is hungry. | You can prepare for a routine feed, but your baby hasn't got the schedule written down. Sometimes it will be hungry at a time you weren't expecting. On these occasions, you have no choice but to let it yell while you get the bottle ready. |
| You may feel uncomfortable breastfeeding a baby in public. | You can comfortably bottle feed a baby just about anywhere – or at least, anywhere you'd go to with a small baby. |
| It is possible to breastfeed a baby while standing up and walking around, but it does nothing for the flow of milk, and most mothers find it impractical except as an occasional emergency measure. | Although both hands are occupied, it is generally easier to bottle feed a baby on the move than to breastfeed it. |
| You can't breastfeed a baby in a moving car, even if you're not the one who is driving, as you both need to be safely strapped in. | In a car a second adult can bottlefeed a baby while they're both strapped into their car seats (potholes help wind the baby). |

# The mother

This is the crux of the issue, really. The best way to feed a baby is whatever way the mother feels happiest with. The stress of breastfeeding a baby when you don't want to will be transmitted to the baby, and the negative effects will outweigh the positive benefits of breastfeeding for the baby. This is why no one but the mother can make the choice. Here are a few factors to consider.

| Breast | Bottle |
|---|---|
| Many mothers love the closeness of breastfeeding their baby, and for some this can outweigh all the negatives. | Some mothers enjoy bottle feeding as much as breastfeeding, and find it an equally close experience. |
| You get your baby all to yourself most of the time if you breastfeed. | You can share the baby-feeding with someone else. |
| It's incredibly convenient having milk constantly on tap regardless of when or where you are. | The first few weeks of parenthood are exhausting enough without adding cleaning, sterilising and making up bottles to your list of chores. |
| Some babies feed around once every four hours and then sleep through for ten hours or more at night. However, a very hungry baby may feed for as much as 18 hours some days (this is right at the extreme). When you're breastfeeding, this doesn't give you much of a break – even going to the loo or cleaning your teeth become quite difficult to arrange. | Formula milk fills babies up better than breast milk so they should spend more time sleeping at night (although they don't come with a guarantee to this effect). When they do need feeding, you can still have a break if you can find someone else to give the baby its bottle. |

| Breast | Bottle |
|---|---|
| It can be difficult – and therefore frustrating and stressful – breastfeeding for the first few days, until you and your baby get the hang of it. | It's easy to bottle feed and you'll have mastered it within a few minutes. |
| Some mothers get very sore nipples between about three and ten days after the baby is born. This can make breastfeeding extremely painful, although nipple shields will ease the problem (but some midwives won't tell you about them because they don't hold with them for some reason). | There are no inherent discomforts associated with bottle feeding and, anyway, you can get someone else to do it. |
| You can never go far without the baby in case it needs you, since no one else can feed it. | You can go out and leave the baby with someone else. |

# The father

It's important not to leave the father out of all this. While it seems logical for the mother to have the casting vote on what kind of milk to give the baby - she's the one who may be getting no sleep, or suffering cracked nipples - the father is the one other person who should have a vote too. (The baby, being under 18, gets no vote at all.)

The father cannot breastfeed the baby. Obvious, but worth saying. This means that he is pretty much excluded from the intimate mother-baby relationship for the first few weeks. Bottle feeding is one solution to this, since the father can share the chores (at three in the morning he may regret voting for this option).

Just as an aside: if you opt for breastfeeding and the father wants an opportunity to bond closely, use a sling whenever you go out and he can carry the baby. Choose one where the baby's head is close to your face so you can make eye contact. This gives father and baby an intimate and special relationship too, as well as giving the mother a break from carrying the baby. Obviously the more often you go out, the stronger the effect will be. New research also shows that both bathing and massaging the baby speeds up the bonding process between father and baby.

# THE PROCESS

There's one key thing to know about making the choice between breast and bottle.

You can start breastfeeding and then switch to the bottle, but you can't start bottle feeding and then change your mind to breastfeeding.

It's not fair, really. It would be far better to try each for a few days and then decide, but you can't do that. Once you stop breastfeeding your milk soon disappears and that's that. So if you think you might prefer to breastfeed, you need to try that option first.

And why can't you do both? Well, in very rare cases a few mothers have successfully combined the two, but it almost never works. You can certainly switch from breast to bottle via a period of maybe a few weeks where you do both, but most mothers eventually stop producing milk if the baby also feeds from a bottle.

It's all the baby's fault, actually. What happens when you breast-feed exclusively is that the baby needs you to produce more milk as it grows. At the end of each breastful, it keeps sucking if it's still hungry, and this signals the system to produce more milk next time. However, if you give the baby a bottle, it soon learns that it doesn't need to keep sucking once the bottle is empty (in fact, it will get wind if it tries it) because you'll either remove the bottle or replace it with a full one. So it gives up the extra sucking for bottle and breast, and the breast is never stimulated to up its output. In fact, since the baby never appears to want any more milk, the system produces slightly less each time.

Some mothers – or babies – can combine breast and bottle feeding indefinitely. This is impossible to predict, however, and by the time you know whether it's working for you, you're committed anyway. If you want or need to introduce mixed feeding, you'd be best waiting until you've been breastfeeding a few months before introducing the bottle. And I'd certainly advise consulting a breastfeeding counsellor about how best to make it work for you.

# EXPRESSING: WHAT'S THAT ABOUT, THEN?

Expressing is a way of feeding breast milk in a bottle. You use a bizarre contraption called a breast pump (definitely not one to try in public) to pump the milk from your breast into a bottle. The point of this is that you can then go out and leave someone else to feed the baby, while still giving it the benefits of a breast milk diet.

If you express only occasionally you may be able to keep the option open indefinitely.

Many mothers, however, start expressing when they return to work so that the baby drinks from a bottle (albeit breast milk) for a large number of feeds. In this case, you're likely to encounter the aforementioned law of diminishing returns with your breast milk production whenever you breastfeed the baby, and may eventually dry up completely.

Having said that, switching to the bottle is the only alternative if you go back to work and leave the baby with someone else, so expressing is a great way to keep both the breastfeeding (when you're at home) and the breast milk going for as long as possible.

## Preparing to breastfeed

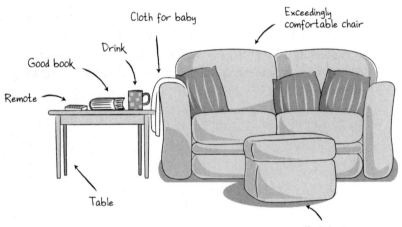

Good book

Remote

Drink

Cloth for baby

Exceedingly
comfortable chair

Table

Footstool

# 4

# Breastfeeding

Once you've made the decision to breastfeed – at least for now – you've done the easy bit. Actually getting the milk to go inside the baby is going to be challenging to begin with. Within a day or two, however, you'll be latching the baby on and off without a second thought.

**Core objective:** Get the milk to go inside the baby

**Key focus:** Have a healthy, happy baby

The interesting thing about starting to breastfeed is that there are two of you learning the skill at the same time. Yep, that's right: the baby has never done it before either. You might think that it's entirely natural and instinctive for the baby. But then, the baby might think the same thing about you. The fact is that you are both aware that you want to bring the baby's mouth into contact with your nipple; how-ever neither of you has actually practised the finer points before. So you have to train the baby as well as yourself on the job.

---

## Myth: breastfeeding is completely instinctive and you ought to be able to do it without any help

This is nonsense. Of course the principle is straightforward and instinctive, and obviously you and the baby would get there in the end if left to your own devices. However, if it takes a few feeds to get into the swing of the thing, this is entirely normal and proper. The vast majority of mothers need help to get off to a good start.

The following guidelines will tell you the basics of how to breastfeed a baby. However, do ask advice from your midwife or anyone else around (who am I kidding? You'll be surrounded by people eager to give you more advice than you could possibly want before you have a chance to ask). These guidelines will help prepare you in advance, and should also help in the middle of the night when there's no one around to give you advice. Moreover, if you give birth when you're snowed in in the Scottish Highlands and the midwife can't reach you, the following advice will be invaluable.

---

# THE PROCESS

1 **Prepare yourself.** OK, this bit isn't essential, but it makes life more pleasant. You're not likely to be going anywhere for at least an hour (unless you really have to), so this is your last decent chance to go to the loo – although this is rarely urgent when you're breastfeeding. It's curious that for the last few months of pregnancy you go to the loo dozens of times a day, and as soon as the baby is born you hardly go again for weeks. All the excess water in your system is going towards making milk. Apart from going to the loo, you might also want to gather your next hour or so's activities around you – a book, a good CD to listen to, the TV remote or whatever. (Remember: no point in trying to do anything which needs more than one hand so leave peeling the potatoes for later.)

2 **Clear the baby's access route.** Until you become adept at this, you'll find it easiest to undo buttons, zips, nursing bras or whatever before you pick the baby up. And breast pads, which you'll need to soak up the leaks. If the baby is yelling, you can always get someone else to pick it up, comfort it, and pass it to you when you're ready. If the father is there, this can be his job.

3 **Get comfortable.** Owing to some strange design flaw, it is not comfortable to feed a baby for any length of time without something to support its weight. If our breasts were further down our chests, the baby would lie comfortably in your lap while you fed it. But they aren't, and it won't. Holding an 8lb weight in the crook of your arm for about an hour is going to get increasingly unpleasant, particularly when you're still not feeling fully fit after the birth.

Use a comfortable chair (you can pick a favourite chair to use every time) and experiment with cushions until you find an arrangement which works. Those big beanbag cushions which wrap right round you are good.

4   **Pick up the baby.** Or get someone to pass it to you. You need to hold it in the crook of your arm so that your upper arm supports its head and your lower arm supports the rest of its body. Your baby is likely to respond to being near its milk supply by doing a sort of rooting around thing which you may find cute. There are other positions you can experiment with such as the reverse of this, where the baby's feet are under your armpit (if you have twins you can do them both at once this way). You can also feed your baby lying on your side in bed, with the baby on the bed and its head cradled in your arm.

5   **Join up the baby with the breast.** Here's where you can't assume first-time success, although you may well be lucky. I'm not trying to depress you, but to let you know that there's no reason to fret if it takes a few minutes to get the baby to cooperate.

What you're aiming for is that the baby should open its mouth wide and attach it around most of the dark areola surrounding the nipple, and then begin to suck firmly.

However, the baby may have other ideas. If it's really yelling, it may not want to stop yelling for long enough to close its mouth round the nipple, for example. Here are a few tips if you have trouble:

○ The baby's mouth should be in line with your nipple – it shouldn't have to twist its neck up, down or sideways to reach.

○ If your baby won't turn its head towards the nipple, try stroking its cheek (the one nearest the breast).

○ If you're having trouble getting it latched on and anyone in the room tries to give you patronising advice, feel free to ask them to leave the room in any language you feel comfortable with.

○ If you and the baby don't manage to find the right position, either the baby will be unable to get enough milk or – more likely – you will get exceedingly sore nipples after a while. So it is essential to get this bit right. Once you're both in the habit of positioning correctly it will quickly become second nature.

6 **Chill.** Once your baby is in position and feeding well, relax and enjoy it. You don't have to do anything else until the baby stops feeding. Ask someone to fetch you a cold drink; don't hold a hot drink over the baby. Get someone else to fix you a sandwich. (Hell, see if you can get anyone spare to fix the leaky roof tile or change a few light bulbs while you're at it.) It's a good idea to drink plenty and keep eating regularly when you're breastfeeding.

Like it or not, you are now housing a small milk production factory and the quality of the milk will be determined by the raw materials you put in.

## A note for fathers

It is easy to feel redundant while your partner is breastfeeding the baby. However, you actually have a vital supporting role to play, and you can make a big difference to their welfare. You can look after the baby while your partner gets comfortable, bring her cups of tea and biscuits, as well as taking the baby for a few minutes to give her a break during a long feed: once its initial hunger is sated a baby will often happily stop feeding for a few minutes, just as you would between courses of a large meal. Also, there is the critical job of winding to be done (we'll get on to winding a couple of chapters later). Every so often your partner can pass you the baby and you can have the fun of seeing if you can get it to burp. For some reason, this seems to be a popular male pastime, and one many men are better at than their partners.

7   **Logging off.** If you want your baby to stop sucking for any reason – perhaps it's in the wrong position and you need to start again – you can't simply pull it away. There's a huge amount of suction there, and you will sorely regret it if you try (and I mean sorely). What you need to do is break the suction, and you do this by sliding your little finger into the baby's mouth alongside your nipple and easing the baby off.

8   **Finishing the feed.** When the baby gets to the end of the breastful of milk, it will continue sucking for a bit just in case there's any more, in much the same way that old people obsessively keep squeezing the toothpaste tube after the toothpaste is finished, just in case they've wasted any. It is this sucking after the milk has finished which notifies your

system that more milk is required next time. So let the baby keep sucking for a bit to ensure your milk production keeps up with its demands – it will unlatch by itself when it realises that there's no more milk for now.

# THE ROUTINE

One baby, two breasts. So how do you dole out the milk effectively?

Your breasts actually dispense two slightly different kinds of milk at each feed. The first to come out is known as the fore milk, and it's runnier and more thirst-quenching than the hind milk, which is richer and more nutritious. Since your baby needs both kinds of milk, it's not a good idea to change breasts until you've emptied the first one otherwise the baby will miss out on the hind milk.

Standard practice, therefore, is to put the baby on one side for one feed and the other side for the next feed. Many babies cooperate with this, but some models refuse to play the game. A hungry baby, for example, will happily empty both at one feed, and still want more (the first one should have refilled by the time the second one is empty). So long as you recognise the need to empty one breast before you start on the next, you should be able to devise your own system for dealing with this kind of variation.

You may find that you can't remember which side you fed the baby on last time, and therefore on which side this feed should be.

Common advice is to tie a ribbon to your bra strap on whichever side you last used. Or should it be on whichever side you are going to use next? And anyway, did you remember to move the ribbon over when you were supposed to? If you can make this system work, or a similar one of your own devising, you may find it helpful. Alternatively, you should be able to judge which breast is fullest – it may, after all, be more than twice the size of the other one. Having established which is fullest, that's the one to use.

# BREASTFEEDING SIDE EFFECTS

There are some interesting experiences associated with breast-feeding, from sore nipples to leaking breasts, which you will never have had the opportunity to discover before. So here's a rundown of some of the most common of them.

- **Leaking.** Sometimes, the milk doesn't know how to stay put. Even when your breasts aren't particularly full, the milk can ooze out. When your baby starts to cry the milk begins to leak out more eagerly. This can also happen when a complete stranger's baby cries, or a baby on the TV, or when you think about your baby, or hear a noise vaguely similar to your baby crying (a cat mewing, for example), or for no apparent reason at all.

At times, the milk can spurt a good couple of feet in front of you, although after a few months this will slow to a trickle.

Breast pads (you can get either disposable or washable ones) will help conceal this from everyone but yourself.

- **Overfilling.** When your breasts get very full, they can become painful. This happens on about day two or three when 'the milk comes in' (as opposed to the yellow colostrum you produce for the first couple of days). It only lasts a couple of days, but it can recur occasionally – usually only briefly – when there's an extended period between feeds. Sooner or later, the baby will decide to sleep for several hours longer than usual and, instead of being grateful for the extra sleep yourself, you'll find yourself in severe pain prodding it to try and get it to wake up and have some milk.

  Occasionally overfull breasts can lead to mastitis, a painful swelling accompanied by fever which is very unpleasant, so you need to do what you can to prevent it.

  When your breasts get sore from being overfull it helps to cool them with a damp flannel, or alternate hot and cold flannels.

  One of the strangest old wives' cures is to put cabbage outer leaves down your bra. Bizarre – but it works. Keep them in the fridge; they're better when they're cold.

- **Refilling.** A few times each day, you'll be aware of a strange sensation almost like a mild electric current running through both breasts at once. This is associated with them refilling with milk. You may or may not like the sensation – it's a matter of opinion really. It reduces after a few months.

- **Sore nipples.** If your nipples get sore and chapped, it can be extremely painful. Get a midwife to help you check that the baby is latched on properly. Insist on advice about nipple shields which – used sparingly – can solve the problem entirely. (Overuse can make it difficult to wean the baby off them later.)

Sore nipples are most common about three days after the baby is born, and often cause women to give up breastfeeding altogether. If you want to persist, it helps to know that you can generally overcome the problem within a few days.

- **Afterpains.** Breastfeeding is part of your body's canny system of healing itself after the birth, since it causes the uterus to contract. For the first few days after the birth, you will find that when you first latch the baby on to feed, it stimulates contractions similar to those of labour though not as strong. These are known as afterpains, and last only a few days, getting less painful all the time.

# Essential equipment for bottle feeding

Bottle   Teat   Teat   Formula milk   Something to
         ring          (comes with own scoop)   sterilise the
                                                  bottles and
                                                  teats in

# 5

# Bottle feeding

If you decide that breastfeeding isn't for you, bottle feeding is the only viable alternative. Instead of putting the milk straight into the baby, you put it in a bottle first and transfer it to the baby from there. Less efficient, yes, but arguably more convenient in the long run.

**Core objective:** Get the milk to go inside the baby

**Key focus:** Have a healthy, happy baby

One of the biggest advantages of bottle feeding the baby is that anyone can do it. Even an older sibling can learn. This means that the father can look after the baby on his own. If you decide to breastfeed, it is hard to emphasise with how stressful it is for the father to be left with a hungry, yelling baby which he has no way of feeding. This way, everyone gets an equal go at playing with the new baby.

---

## Myth: bottle feeding is better because you can see how much milk the baby is drinking

You can indeed, but unless your baby is severely underweight or ill this really isn't important. Your baby will drink as much as it needs to, and so long as it is healthy and happy you don't need to fret about it.

---

# THE KIT

There are certain essentials for bottle feeding a baby, which can seem a bit daunting when you first set out to buy the equipment. Make sure you have stocked up with the basics before the baby is born. All you will really need is:

- **Bottles.** These come in several shapes but they all do the same job. They come with screw-on caps to hold the teat in place, and lids to keep the teat sterile once the bottle is made up. They generally come with teats, too, but you can buy the teats separately. The baby is likely to get through about eight feeds a day so if you have only two bottles, you'll have to sterilise about four times a day.

- **Teats.** These come with different sized holes to suit different sized babies. You need to check the size when you buy them (whether they come with the bottle or on their own). You're looking for something that says 'newborn' on it or something similar.

- **Formula milk.** There are two or three leading brands. What's important is that you look at the tin to see what age the formula is suitable for. Some tins have strange names like 'follow-on milk' but you want the one which says it's suitable for newborns.

There are lots of other optional pieces of equipment such as fancy sterilisers and bottle warmers, but you can manage without them all if you prefer, or if your budget is tight. Even sterilising can be done perfectly well with just a pan of boiling water.

# THE PROCESS

1 **Keep everything sterile.** The next chapter is about sterilising so I won't go into detail here. Suffice to say that when your baby is tiny you need to pretend that you're in a sci-fi movie where everyone is going round in those white anti-radiation suits. No germs must come into contact with anything that goes inside the baby. So you need to start the process with sterile milk, water, measuring spoon, bottle, teat and everything else. Then you touch everything with your hands, so you need to have cleaned them too.

If you are of a robust disposition, you might wonder how the baby is ever going to build up any resistance to germs in this way. I have wondered this myself. But better safe than sorry. However, if you remember half way through the feed that you forgot to wash your hands before assembling the bottle, don't panic. The chances of this doing your baby any harm this once are virtually nil. Just try to remember next time. Anyway, make sure you always have sterile stuff ready for the next feed, or you'll have to listen to a lot of crying while you spend 15 or 20 minutes sterilising everything and then cooling it all down.

2 **Recognise when it's feeding time.** Tiny babies often feed every two hours or so (for about an hour at a time) so at any given moment it could need feeding. Basically, if it cries and hasn't been fed for a while, chances are it's hungry. If it doesn't cry, it isn't hungry.

3 **Make up the feed.** You need to follow the instructions on the tin, but this will usually involve putting a certain amount of sterile water (ie water which has been boiled and then cooled down) in the bottle and then adding the milk powder. Don't use bottled mineral water as it can contain unhealthy levels of minerals for a baby (and using fizzy by mistake instead of still would lead to the kind of wind that doesn't bear thinking about). Equally, you should avoid water which contains water softeners. It is important to get the right ratio of powder to water – too much water and the baby won't get sufficient nourishment; too much milk powder and the baby might get ill. Shake the mixture thoroughly to remove all lumps.

You can buy ready mixed cartons of milk. They are pretty expensive, but can be useful if you're travelling. Don't give the baby cow's milk or goat's milk or anything else that isn't specifically formulated for human babies.

4  **Get the milk to the right temperature.** There is a myth that babies need their milk to be at body temperature, the same as breast milk. In fact, they need it to be no hotter than this (or it could burn them) and no colder than room temperature. Anything in between is fine. You can buy fancy milk warmers, but frankly it's just as easy to heat up a bottle by standing it in a bowl of hot water.

Before you administer the milk to the baby, check the temperature by squirting a little bit on to a sensitive part of your skin such as your wrist. If the milk doesn't feel hot to you, it is at or below body temperature and will do fine.

5  **Get ready to feed.** Once the milk is ready, you need a baby to complete the operation. First prepare a comfortable place to sit, along with any music you want to listen to or anything else to occupy you (remember: no free hands), and then collect the baby. Hold the baby in one arm, its head resting on the upper arm.

6  **Put the squishy end of the bottle in the baby's mouth.** If the baby seems vague about what's going on, you can stroke the cheek nearest to you to encourage it to open its mouth and start rooting around. Then gently put the teat in its mouth, making sure it is well in and the baby is sucking strongly, not simply gumming the teat as if it were some kind of infant chewing gum. Before long, it will cooperate fully with this procedure. You need to make sure that the end of the bottle the baby drinks from is full of milk so no air can get into the teat. The baby does not want to suck air. This is very easy to start with but as the bottle empties you will need to angle it up to make sure the teat still contains only milk.

7   **Keep going.** Once you're both comfortable, just carry on until one of the following happens: the milk is finished, the baby has had enough, or the baby needs winding (see page 6).

8   **Stop.** When it's time to stop, you may need to unlatch the baby from the teat. Slip your little finger into the baby's mouth alongside the teat to break the suction, and then you can easily slide the bottle out of its mouth. Or the baby may stop by itself. You don't have to get the baby to empty the bottle every time; it will drink as much milk as it wants and then stop, just as you would.

Sometimes the teat collapses as the baby's suction starts to create a vacuum inside the bottle. Take the bottle out of its mouth and loosen the top slightly to allow air back in. The teat will spring back into shape. Tighten the lid again and carry on from step 5.

---

## Giving extra water

If the weather is very hot, a formula-fed baby may need extra water. Boil it first to sterilise it, and then cool it down before giving it to the baby. Put it in a bottle just as you do the formula milk. The thing to avoid here is filling the baby up with water instead of milk, so don't give the water as a replacement for a bottle feed, and give it in small quantities at a time.

---

# SAYING NO TO GERMS

Hygiene around the baby's feeding stuff is important. It's true that lots of babies all over the world survive with no sterilising equipment at all and always have done (although most of them are breastfed). But you significantly increase the chances of illness if you don't sterilise, especially with a newborn baby. Here are a few basic guidelines:

- The most critical thing to avoid giving your baby is any trace of old milk which may have gone bad, as this will harbour germs. Clean bottles and teats thoroughly, and sterilise them every time.

- Once you warm up the milk you create an ideal breeding ground for those dratted germs. So if you then don't use the milk for any reason, don't reuse it later. Throw it away.

- Even if all your equipment is sterile, don't give the baby milk you have warmed for over an hour, as germs will have had time to breed.

- You can store milk (that hasn't been warmed) in a refrigerator for up to 24 hours; it's certainly worth preparing night time bottles in advance.

- Throw away any leftover or unused milk at the end of a feed.

# Cross-section of baby with wind

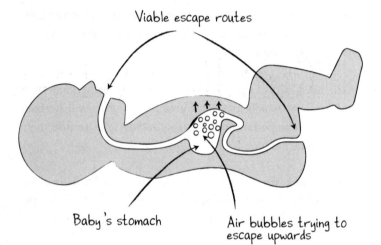

Viable escape routes

Baby's stomach

Air bubbles trying to
escape upwards

Tip the baby up to release
the trapped air bubbles

# 6

# Tackling wind

You've almost certainly heard about winding babies but what does it actually mean? When are you supposed to do it, and how? Winding is one of those total mysteries which suddenly becomes clear within the first few days of the baby being born.

**Core objective:** Remove the excess air from the baby

**Key focus:** Don't damage the baby

For some reason babies take in air with their milk even though you didn't give it to them and they didn't actually want it. Then they decide they don't like it, so they want to let it back out – the way you might feel after downing a whole glass of something fizzy. However babies, although sometimes capable of burping impressively, often need help to be able to burp. Yep, winding is simply the genteel term for burping the baby.

## Myth: winding the baby is an optional activity

I knew a couple who were miserable by the time their baby was a few weeks old. It seemed healthy and happy, but it started crying and whinging within a few minutes of starting a feed and, although it was a heavy baby, it never seemed to feed enough and kept breaking off from its milk. They were both exhausted (never getting enough milk the baby wasn't sleeping much) and getting very crabby with each other. When I asked if it might be wind they replied, 'Oh, no. We never wind it. Don't believe in all that stuff.'

# THE PROCESS

1   **Recognise when the baby has wind.** There's no point aimlessly winding the baby just because you're looking for something to do. Either a baby needs winding or it doesn't. You need to learn when it does. For a start, it's something that happens during feeds, or sometimes at the end of a feed. The only other thing that occasionally causes wind is a lot of serious crying.

Supposedly babies get less windy if they're breastfed but, if you do breastfeed, you might find this hard to believe.

Some babies are windier than others, but they all determinedly get wind several times each feed no matter how you feed them. The signs are:

- The baby keeps breaking off from feeding.

- It starts crying.

- It tries to latch on again as though it's hungry, but it doesn't actually last long before breaking off again.

- It may go white around the edges of the mouth.

2   **Stop feeding.** This is easy, because the baby will already have become detatched from the nipple or teat. If it's still happily feeding, it doesn't need winding yet. Wait until it breaks off by itself.

3   **Get the baby to burp.** Aha, that's the tricky bit. If the mother is breastfeeding, this is a great job for the father. It gives the mother a break and the father gets to spend some time with the baby and make it happy again. There are various techniques you can try:

- Sometimes just sitting the baby up does the trick. Air will always go upwards, so the idea is to give it an easy upward route out of the baby.

- Sit the baby on your lap and pat it on the back. This is intended to loosen the air bubbles in the baby's stomach and send them back up. If you tap the baby too gently it won't work; however you obviously don't want to slap the baby too violently either. You need to be firm so experiment, starting gently and gradually patting a little more strongly as you can tell that the baby is OK with it.

○ Rest the baby upright (head uppermost and facing you) against your shoulder and pat it on the back. It's advisable to put a cloth over your shoulder and down your back as you do this, as this is where the baby will put the sick.

○ You can lie the baby across your lap with its tummy on one knee and its head on the other, turned away from you (it needs to be able to breathe while you wind it). Now pat it on the back. Sometimes, even if this doesn't work, turning the baby upright afterwards does the trick and frees up those pesky air bubbles.

○ You can also try swinging the baby very gently back and forth. You do this by lying it face down along your lower arm with your hand facing up and supporting its head. Use your other hand to help support it and hold it close to you. The gentle movement may help dislodge the air.

**4  Don't let the baby lull you into a false sense of security.**

Winding can sometimes take ten seconds and the baby will go happily back to feeding again. At other times it can take up to ten or 15 minutes to get the air up.

Or the baby will burp once and give you no indication that that was only the first tremor heralding the main event in a few minutes time. For this reason winding can be slightly frustrating unless you approach it as an enjoyable exercise in itself. It's easy to feel at times that this is the baby's idea of a joke, teasing you on purpose and challenging you to see if you can actually get that last bubble of air out. All the medical evidence indicates that the baby is as much an innocent victim as you in this process; but you'll still suspect it at times.

5 **Clean up as necessary.** You can't assume that when the air finally comes up it will come alone. It may well be accompanied by milk – frequently more milk than you think the baby has actually drunk (it's an optical illusion). This is commonly known as being sick. To be fair, baby sick really isn't as yucky as older sick, but you'll still find that you need a bib on the baby and/or a cloth to hand.

6 **Revert to feeding mode.** Well done, you've successfully winded the baby and can continue the feed. If the feed has finished and the baby is due to go to sleep, that last winding session will have thoroughly woken it up. This is just one of those things – it happens to the most experienced parents so don't feel bad about it. The milk is supposed to send it to sleep but it won't sleep if it's windy, and you wake it up if you do anything about it. If you find a foolproof solution to this one, please let me know. Otherwise you just have to get it to sleep with some more milk, or by some other method.

Successful winding is all about trial and error. You'll probably find that your baby responds better to one method than another. Every few weeks, the best method may change. Some babies will even happily go to sleep without any winding at all.

# Equipment to sterilise

Bottle    Teat ring    Teat    Bottle    Dummy    Spoon    Bowl

(thing that attaches teat to bottle)     lid

If it touches the baby's food or mouth, keep it sterile

# 7

# Sterilising

Although a lot of baby equipment is quite unnecessary, you do need to sterilise bottle feeding equipment. If you don't, the bacteria in any traces of old milk left in the bottle could make the baby ill. One of the advantages of breastfeeding is that you get to skip this whole chapter, at least until the baby is ready for solid food.

**Core objective:** Get the bottle feeding equipment germ-free

**Key focus:** Don't let the baby get ill

You need to sterilise all bottle feeding equipment until the baby stops drinking milk from a bottle. When you wean it onto solid food (that just means if it starts eating solid foods), you'll need to sterilise bowls and spoons as well until it's about a year old. You'll need to check that the ones you buy can be sterilised without melting – the label should tell you.

## Myth: you've got to have a proper steriliser

Actually, a large pan of boiling water does the job just as well as a proper steriliser.

# THE PROCESS

1  **Clean everything.** The first thing to do is wash everything up as you would normally. Sterilisers don't do that bit for you (if they did they'd have to make them large enough to fit all your pots and pans in too). Use warm soapy water and make sure you get into the nooks and crannies in teats and bottles to clean off all traces of milk. You might find a small teat brush handy for this (you can usually buy them from the baby food aisle), but you can manage without. Use fresh clean water for this – not the same bowl of water you just washed the roasting pan in.

2  **Rinse it.** The baby doesn't want to drink washing up liquid, even if it's sterile. So give the stuff a good rinse before you sterilise it.

3 **Put it in the steriliser.** There are three main methods of sterilising, and you'll need to follow the manufacturer's instructions if you're using a proper steriliser.

○ **Boiling water.** If you don't have a proper steriliser, simply put your clean equipment in a large pan of water with a lid. Make sure the bottles and teats are submerged as far as possible. Bring the water to the boil and boil it for a good ten minutes. Then leave everything to cool down with the lid still on.

○ **Chemical sterilisers.** These use cold water with tablet or liquid sterilising chemicals dissolved in it. The solution has to be changed regularly. Once the solution is made up you add the equipment – submerging it as much as possible and leaving no air pockets – and leave it for however long the instructions tell you to. Having done this, the equipment now has traces of chemicals on it so you need to rinse it all off with water. That's sterile water, of course. This means boiled water which has cooled down.

○ **Steam sterilisers.** These are designed to go on the stove or in a microwave, or you can get electric models which sit on the worktop and plug in. They all have lids and work by using a small amount of water in a reservoir below the equipment, which is boiled so that the equipment is surrounded by the hot steam. Since steam naturally rises, bottles, bowls etc have to go in upside down so the steam can get inside them.

4 **Take the equipment out.** You don't have to do this straight away, but sooner or later you'll need to use the stuff. In fact, don't do it too soon, except with a chemical steriliser, or you'll burn yourself.

Before you get the stuff out, think through what you're going to do with it. If you put it down somewhere that isn't clean, you might as well go back and repeat the whole process.

Obviously you can stand the bottle on a clean work surface while you make up the next feed. But if you put the teat down on the chopping board you've just been using... back you go to start again. If in doubt, put equipment down on clean kitchen paper.

There's no need to take the equipment out of the pan or steriliser at all until you need to use it. However, you can't leave it in there indefinitely and expect it to stay sterile for days.

As a guide, aim to sterilise twice a day, so nothing has been sitting in the steriliser for more than a few hours.

Since most sterilisers hold only six bottles, and your baby will probably be on at least eight feeds a day to begin with, you can see that this is a sensible system to aim for.

# Nappy changing starting position

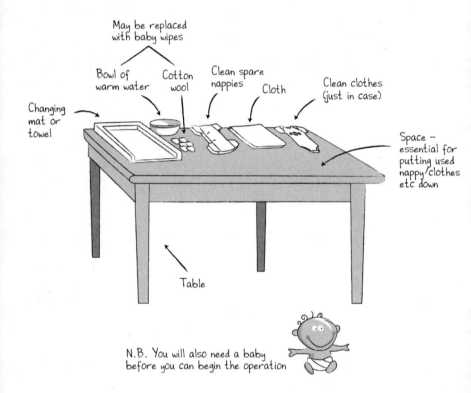

May be replaced
with baby wipes

Bowl of
warm water

Cotton
wool

Clean spare
nappies

Cloth

Clean clothes
(just in case)

Changing
mat or
towel

Space –
essential for
putting used
nappy/clothes
etc down

Table

N.B. You will also need a baby
before you can begin the operation

# Changing the nappy

Babies, like humans, have to perform excretory functions. Once you have a baby, you must refer to these functions as peeing and poohing. These excretions can be conveniently captured in a nappy – a flexible and, ideally, waterproof item which wraps neatly around the baby's bottom.

**Core objective:** Replace the dirty nappy with a clean one

**Key focus:** Contain the used pooh in the old nappy, rather than redistributing it around the baby

Several variations on the nappy theme are available, but there are no variations on the general baby model. They all pee and pooh, and they all have occasions when they do it excessively. The important thing, however, is to exchange each nappy for a clean one every so often.

A strong smell of pooh is always a clear sign that now would be a good time to change the baby's nappy...!

You're aiming to improve the general hygiene levels around the baby, so the whole exercise is a bit pointless if everyone ends up covered in pooh. This may well happen round about the mid stage of the process; this is par for the course. The important thing is that you keep going until you've cleaned up the bulk of it.

---

## Myth: changing a nappy is a piece of piss once you know what you're doing

Don't let people tell you this; it will simply make you feel inadequate. You will certainly find that, as you become more practised, the exercise often seems simple. But every so often your baby will deliver a truly challenging nappy. Even the most experienced and talented parents get covered in pooh sometimes.

---

# THE OPTIONS

It's necessary to say a few words about the bewildering array of nappy changing options that confronts parent. Trickiest of all is the nappies themselves. Do you go for reusable ones or disposable ones? Actually, this is a trick question. And the reason it's a trick is because there is no right answer. So don't sweat it. You can ask other parents, and read up on it, but in the end just choose what suits you. The important thing is that they all do the same job, and they all do it fine. Here's a quick guide to the key points about each type:

- **Reusables:** more cash up front because you have to buy quite a lot of gear. Should work out cheaper over time unless your baby is potty trained within a few months (note: this isn't normal). Certainly cheaper if you can pass the nappies on to a subsequent child but, really, would you want to? On the downside, bear in mind that you do have to clean them before you can reuse them. This is yucky if you're squeamish about such things, and is also time consuming.

- **Disposables:** much more expensive over time, but you only spend the money a bit at a time, so maybe you won't notice. Not good for the environment (they take years to break down in landfill sites); even the eco-friendly ones are worse news than reusables for landfill. On the other hand, there's less water and energy used in laundering so the reusable ones aren't all they're cracked up to be environmentally either. Less likely to leak or give the baby a rash. They are quick and easy to use, and easy to dispose of (hence the term 'disposables').

Once you've made this basic choice, there's still an enormous range to select from. I can't help you here. All I can tell you is that there's not much to choose and the baby is in no position to complain that you've got it wrong, so you can get away with pretty much anything.

The other main choice you'll need to make is whether to clean your baby with wipes or with cotton wool and water. Basically, wipes are easier, but they give some babies a rash. Cotton wool and warm water is harmless and cheaper, but marginally more hassle. Again, unless your baby chooses to react badly to wipes, it's up to you.

# THE EQUIPMENT

- **A place.** You have to change the baby's nappy somewhere. Many parents have a designated place, perhaps in the bedroom or the bathroom, but you can of course change the baby anywhere you like. You can even change it in a different place each time if you want to – God knows the nappy changing routine could do with some variety. Most parents also choose to use a changing mat or some variation on this. It's entirely unnecessary, although you can have one if you want. Equally, you could just chuck a towel down under the baby so it doesn't get too cold or uncomfortable (they don't like being cold or uncomfortable). When it gets covered in pooh you can fling it in the wash (the towel, that is).

- **Cotton wool or wipes.** Don't let a few manageable nappies lull you into a false sense of security. Every so often, a nappy will come along that requires about half a pound of cotton wool or half a packet of wipes for the clean-up operation.

- **Clean nappies.** For the purposes of the following guide, I shall assume you are using disposables. If you are using reusables, you'll need to get folding/pinning/tying off instructions for the particular nappy you're using. Don't expect the baby to remember how you did it up last time.

Expect to get through about six to eight nappies a day to begin with, reducing to three or four by the time it's a few months old (they pooh less often once they're on solid food).

- **Nappy sacks.** By no means compulsory, but they do keep the smell in. Put the stinking nappies in a nappy sack before you throw them away and the bin won't smell (they're great for putting onion peelings into before throwing them away, too). If you want to economise, and save the planet at the same time, you can always use old supermarket carrier bags instead.

- **Cloth or clean rag.** This is for emergencies (see later).

## A word about creams

Some people put what they call a barrier cream on the baby's bottom before doing up the new nappy. It's supposed to stop the pee and pooh getting into the baby's skin and giving it a nappy rash. In fact, you shouldn't use it routinely with disposable nappies as it prevents the urine soaking into the nappy and away from the skin. Since the next chapter is about nappy rash anyway, and since it shouldn't be necessary to use a cream routinely, I shan't include it in the following guide to changing a nappy.

# THE PROCESS

1 **Get everything ready.** It is difficult to emphasise strongly enough how very sorry you will be if you open up a nappy overflowing with runny pooh and then realise that you haven't got any wipes to hand (for 'wipes' read 'cotton wool or wipes'). Resealing the nappy is an option, but it's not a good one. It tends to exacerbate the problem for next time you open it. So have wipes, nappy sacks and clean nappies ready.

2 **Fetch the baby.** This process requires a baby, so go and get it. Put it down in the place you have selected. It should be face up. Once it is a few months old, by the way, it will learn that the first thing to do when you open a nappy full of pooh is to stick its hands in it. When it reaches this stage, part of the preparation entails putting something interesting and absorbing into its hands to distract it (that's absorbing, not absorbent).

3 **Remove the baby's clothing as necessary.** You may now find that you can't actually see the nappy, let alone reach it. This is because the baby is wearing clothes over the top of it. Remove any clothing you need to in order to get at the nappy comfortably.

Don't bother removing clothes you don't need to; life's too short.

You will need to remove the baby's shoes as it is easier to clean pooh off feet than off shoes.

4   **Undo the nappy.** Pulling the front part down, peer carefully inside to see what you're dealing with. Be prepared for the contents to be any colour from black and treacly for the first few days, to anything from mustard yellow to green. If necessary, pull the front part back up and hold it in place while you summon the will to continue. Once you're ready to proceed, pull the front part back down, using it to wipe off any significant areas of pooh as it goes. It should come to rest on top of the inside back part of the nappy so the pooh is still contained, so far at least.

5   **Raise the baby's bottom.** You need to get the baby's bottom up in the air so you can get at everything you need to. The way to lift a baby's bottom is to take hold of both ankles with one hand and lift them (you should always treat a baby gently; they can be fragile). This causes the legs to follow on, and eventually the bottom will be raised up.

6   **Wipe the pooh or pee off.** Use the wipes to clean the baby's skin. If you have a girl baby you need to wipe from front to back to avoid transferring any infection to the vagina. Even if there's no pooh, you still need to clean off the pee (yes, I know it's invisible) so it doesn't make the baby sore. This process can take anything between one and about 30 wipes or lumps of cotton wool, but it's usually under 10. As each wipe reaches capacity and needs replacing, you can simply put the used one on top of the folded over nappy.

7   **Make sure you've got it all covered.** Babies are born with few skills. They cannot walk, talk or even chew gum. They can, however, pooh down their legs, up their backs and right round their tummies in a way that you would hesitate to compete with. So make sure you've found all the pooh, including cleaning all the cracks and crevices. (If things get

really bad, abandon the whole nappy change, strip the baby and clean it in a bath – see page 10).

8 **Remove the nappy.** When you have finished (or possibly part way through if you're using a lot of wipes) you will need to extract the nappy from underneath the baby. The aim is to raise the baby's bottom again by lifting its legs, roll the nappy in on itself a little way to contain the wipes and the pooh, and then deftly whisk the nappy out. If you're using disposables, beware the sticky tabs at the top don't adhere to the baby's skin, or you'll find the nappy won't budge and the pooh is likely to be distributed over a wider area than you'd intended. Always release the tabs first.

9 **Render the nappy safe.** Finish rolling the nappy in on itself, and then use the sticky tabs to seal it shut. Put it in the nappy sack if you're using one, and tie it off. You can now breathe a sigh of relief.

10 (optional) **Clean the baby again.** When you turn back to the baby, you may well find that it has waited until you completely removed the nappy before doing another pee or pooh. It's just something they do – all that fresh air makes them pee. In this case, repeat steps 5 to 10, and make a mental note to put the fresh nappy on as quickly as possible next time. If you catch the baby peeing while its nappy is off, this is the time to use the emergency cloth (especially on male babies, who will pee straight up in the air). Clamp the cloth firmly over the flow of pee until it has subsided.

11 (optional) **Pick the baby up off the floor.** Another thing that can happen when you turn away is that your baby rolls off the table. This is bad. Very bad. When they're tiny, babies can't do this, but some can manage it by as young as three

or four months. Several preventive solutions are possible; in particular you can keep one hand on the baby while you dispose of the nappy, or you can adopt the blindingly simple technique of changing the baby on the floor.

12 **Put the clean nappy on the baby.** Before you do this, work out which way round it goes. The sticky tabs go on the bit which slides underneath the baby, and there's usually a picture on the nappy to show you which is the outside. (If you're using reusables, you're on your own.) Slide the back of the nappy under the baby's bottom, using the ankle lift technique to raise the bottom, until the top of it is level with the baby's waist. Lower the legs and bring the front of the nappy between the legs so the top of this end also reaches to the waist. Hold the front of the nappy down, peel back the sticky tabs, and bring these tabs round the sides of the baby one at a time to stick down over the front section of the nappy.

13 **Replace the clothing.** Don't forget to put the baby's clothes back on, or, if they are now designated for the wash, find some clean clothes to put on it.

Well done; you now have between about two minutes and four hours before you have to repeat the process.

# Preventing nappy rash

Baby's bottom with frequent exposure to fresh air and clean nappies

Baby's bottom after long term imprisonment in soiled nappies

# Tackling nappy rash

Nappy rash is a red rash or red raised spots which appear around a baby's bottom and in the folds of skin around the tops of its legs. Identifying it is pretty straightforward, but what we're after here is getting rid of it.

**Core objective:** Get rid of the rash

**Key focus:** Keep the baby comfortable and happy

While nappy rash isn't pleasant for the baby, neither is it dangerous. In fact, babies often seem to put up with a very severe looking rash with no complaint at all except when you change their nappy, which is an uncomfortable process for them. This doesn't mean you should ignore it; simply that you shouldn't worry about it unduly.

## Myth: if your baby gets nappy rash you haven't been looking after it properly

If this is true, it's bad news for all of us since I've rarely encountered a baby that hasn't had nappy rash at some time. It's true that if you persistently neglect the baby – or at least the nappy changing part of it – it's bound to get nappy rash. However even the most diligent and experienced parents' babies get it occasionally.

# THE CAUSES

Nappy rash is caused by too little air getting at the baby's bottom, combined with too much moisture and too many chemicals of the kind found in urine and faeces (and more so with formula milk than with breast milk). In fact the combination of these two is particularly prone to irritate the skin, which is one reason why you should change a poohy nappy straight away (the other reason being that you can't stand the smell any longer).

Disposable nappies do have the edge here, since they draw the moisture into the centre and away from the skin. However, with more frequent nappy changes you can perfectly well reduce nappy rash with reusables too.

If you think about it, the human body was never designed to have urine and pooh clamped to the bottom by means of an airtight constraint, so it's hardly surprising that it can cause problems. The solutions all lie in minimising this effect: getting more air to the skin and not allowing the pee or pooh – and especially the two in combination – to stay close to the skin for prolonged periods.

If you catch nappy rash early enough, you can get rid of it in a few hours. Once it becomes severe (and this can happen before you've had a chance to catch it) it may take a few days. However you should still be able to see an improvement within hours.

# THE PROCESS

1   **Recognise the nappy rash.** When you change the baby's nappy look out for signs of redness. If the rash gets bad you can't miss it, but spotting it early means you can clear it up faster.

Apart from the occasional redness caused by a tight nappy, which will fade quickly, almost every case of redness, soreness or rash in the nappy vicinity is nappy rash – the only other common complaint you might confuse it with is thrush.

(Having said that, you should of course seek medical advice if it persists, or if you have any concerns that it may be something else).

2  **Clean the baby's bottom thoroughly.** If you use baby wipes these may make the rash sting. If the baby reacts badly to the wipes use cotton wool and warm water to clean it. Even if it looks clean, you still need to remove all traces of urine so clean it anyway. Bathing the baby at this juncture is also helpful (see page 10), though not compulsory. It will both clean it up and ease the discomfort.

3  **Let the air get at it.** This helps more than anything else. So let your baby go without a nappy for as long as you can. Be smart here. If your baby has no nappy on there will be no way of neatly capturing anything that may emanate from its nether regions. So put it on a waterproof sheet, lie it down in the shade out of doors in good weather, or find some other way to anticipate the inevitable effectively. You can always just cover the main danger areas loosely in a cloth.

4  **Consider using creams.** You can probably cure mild nappy rash with a good session of airing. A more severe rash may need cream applied to it. You can buy creams for nappy rash or, if it persists, your doctor or health visitor may prescribe something stronger – certainly you should ask advice from a doctor, health visitor or midwife if the rash is reluctant to disappear.

5  **Put a fresh nappy on.** Sooner or later you'll have to put a nappy back on the baby. Maybe you have to go out in five minutes, or perhaps it's feeding or nap time. If you use reusable nappies it will help to use a barrier cream to protect the baby's bottom. However this is not only unnecessary with disposable nappies but arguably makes them less effective as they already contain protective oils.

6 **Change the nappy frequently.** Yes, I'm afraid that favourite parental occupation has to be stepped up for a while. The more frequently you change the nappy, the faster the nappy rash will go. As a rough guide, change it after every feed as well as any time your nose tells you that it needs changing.

# Bathing the baby
## List of ingredients

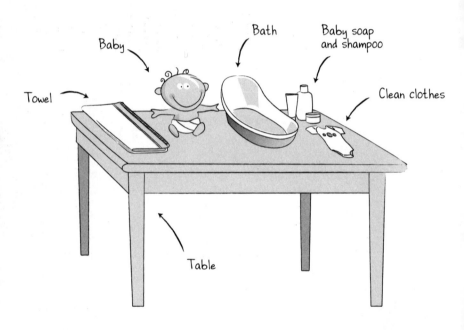

Baby

Bath

Baby soap and shampoo

Towel

Clean clothes

Table

All the ingredients may be left unattended
EXCEPT the baby

# 10
# Bathtime

Sooner or later, you're going to notice some grubbiness around the baby's ears, maybe, or perhaps between the toes. At this point you will think to yourself, 'Ah. I should make this baby cleaner than it is now. I wonder how I'm going to do that.' The answer is that you're going to give it a bath.

**Core objective:** Clean the baby

**Key focus:** Don't drown the baby

So long as the baby comes out of this process alive and as healthy as it went into it, you haven't failed. If it also comes out cleaner than it started, you've successfully bathed it. Anything else is icing on the cake. For example, if all of it is cleaner than before, instead of just some bits, you're really rocking and rolling.

---

## Myth: you need to buy a special baby bath for your baby

This is nonsense. You can perfectly well bath a baby in the sink (just mind its head on the taps), in a bucket, or in any other clean object which it fits into and which holds water.

---

# THE PROCESS

1  **Prepare the bath.** The first thing to do when you bath your baby is to get the bath ready. If you get the baby ready first, you will find yourself wondering where to put it while you sort out the bath. This doesn't really matter, but if you don't want it to pee everywhere you'll end up putting half its clothes back on again. Harmless but pointless.

2  **Get the temperature sorted out.** The bath shouldn't be too hot or too cold. Babies are more sensitive to temperature than you are. You can stick your elbow in it if you think that will help. Otherwise use your common sense – somewhere around lukewarm is what you're aiming for.

3  **Get all the other stuff ready too.** Get some cleaning stuff ready – soap or shampoo or whatever. It's easier to use something you can manage with one hand, such as

liquid rather than solid soap. Actually you can perfectly well wash a baby's hair with soap, or its skin with baby shampoo so don't get hung up on this. If you've forgotten the soap and the shampoo, just wash it in plain water. No one will find out.

4   **Don't forget the towel.** Next, get stuff for after the bath ready: a towel, fresh nappy and clothes. Talcum powder is completely unnecessary, but you're welcome to use it if it makes you happy. If you don't get all this ready you will still have achieved your core objective (cleaning the baby) and your key focus (not drowning it), so you're doing OK, but the baby might get cold while you dig out a towel.

5   **Get the baby ready.** Now remove all the baby's clothes. If you don't, bits of your baby won't get properly clean. Obviously the baby will prefer you to do this in a reasonably warm room.

6   **Hold the baby.** Follow the instructions earlier in the book (page 2). And keep hold of it. This is all to do with the not drowning it stuff. So long as you hold on to your baby constantly it is all but impossible to drown it. If you have to leave the bath at any time, for example to answer the phone, take the baby with you so you can keep holding on to it. Or don't answer the phone. It's a simple matter of priorities: ignore the phone or drown the baby? Think it through.

7   **Wash the baby's hair.** Standard procedure is to hold the baby with one arm so it is out of the water, maybe wrapped in a towel (if you don't fancy being peed on), and lower its head until it is close to the water (that's close, not under). It should be facing upwards, looking towards you. Now you can use your other hand to wash the baby's hair. Gravity will prevent

the water from getting onto its face. If you remembered the shampoo, so much the better. Just a little squeeze of it is fine – there isn't an exact right amount.

8   **...or don't.** Sometimes, you may find you've clean forgotten to wash the baby's hair before you put it in the bath. Ah, well. There's always next time. Or you could improvise with the baby already in the water.

9   **Clean the baby.** Once you've rinsed off the baby's hair, you can turn it the right way up and put it in the bath (remove the towel first if you were using it).

Remember to keep hold of it. If you put one arm behind the baby's back and grip it under the far arm, this leaves the other hand free to wash it.

If you are using a proper baby bath, you may find this exercise extremely slippery. If you're using the sink or a bucket it will probably be much easier. For the first few days the remains of your baby's end of the umbilical cord will still be attached and drying out. This will fall off naturally, usually within about a fortnight of the birth. Until then you need to clean it with warm water, and then dry it off well.

10  **Stop.** When you've finished bathing the baby, take it out of the water. You'll know when this happens because either the baby will start yelling (if it ever stopped), or your arm will start to ache, or you'll just get bored. The objective was to clean the baby so if you sense it is now cleaner than it was before, you can stop.

11 **Dry it and dress it.** Wrap the baby in the towel. When it is dry you can get it dressed. If you don't fancy drying all the cracks and crevices, leave the baby in the towel to dry out naturally. (Just make sure it's properly dry before you dress it.) So long as you're holding it, it will be quite happy.

There are few things pleasanter to hold than a small baby wrapped in a towel just out of its bath. Congratulations: you have successfully bathed your baby.

# Baby clothes to avoid

This is the garment the baby will choose to be sick on EVERY TIME

... or this one

Any one-piece item of clothing which doesn't popper under the crotch will have to be removed in its entirety in order to change the baby's nappy

If it's barely big enough now, the baby will out grow it within days

Avoid small necks. If it won't slip easily over the baby's head, you don't want it

If it needs ironing, forget it

# Dressing the baby

Unless you live in a very hot country, or are a committed naturist with powerful central heating, you're going to have to put some clothes on the baby. The object of the exercise is to ensure the baby is comfortable, and not too hot or too cold.

**Core objective:** Make the baby warm enough

**Key focus:** Don't break it

Contrary to popular opinion, you can put pink clothes on a boy, black clothes on a girl (if you can find any), or in fact any clothes on any baby so long as they do the job of making it warm and comfortable. Babies aren't sticklers for fashion, and you can get away with putting them in any style of clothes without hearing a word of complaint from them.

## Myth: a baby must have a vest

This sounds like something out of the thirties. Of course babies don't need vests. Human infants have not evolved to require a vest in order to thrive. Vests serve a useful purpose, and many parents choose to use them, but plenty of happy, healthy babies have never worn vests.

# CHOOSING CLOTHES

I have no idea what your personal taste is in baby clothes and I wouldn't presume to tell you what you should and shouldn't choose. However, you might like to bear in mind the following points:

- Baby clothes come in certain basic sizes: newborn, up to one month, 0–3 months and so on. If your baby is average to large it will grow out of anything less than 0–3 months almost instantly.

  If you don't want to spend a fortune, opt for clothes which say they'll fit for up to three months unless you know your baby is going to be small.

- For ease of putting on and taking off, you want clothes with necks which will easily stretch to go over the baby's head (assuming they go on this way).

- Make sure that jumpsuits and babygrow type things (that's all-in-one stuff) popper under the crotch. Otherwise you'll have to remove the entire garment – arms and all – every time you want to change the nappy.

Anything which you can't just chuck in a washing machine is likely to be more trouble than it's worth.

- All those guides which tell you how many of everything you need probably aren't kidding. Unless you want to be doing washing round the clock, you need several changes of basic clothes. Some days the baby will go all day in the same outfit. Another day, for some whimsical reason of its own, it will either puke down several tops in a row, or leak out of each nappy in turn, requiring several changes of clothes.

You should never, ever, ever need to iron baby clothes!

# GENERAL GUIDELINES

You may be concerned about hurting the baby. Don't worry – just follow these guidelines. Of course you need to be gentle, but babies the world over survive being dressed and undressed perfectly well, and this one should be no exception.

- Take care not to let any of its fingers or thumbs get bent backwards.

- Think about which way human joints are able to bend and don't expect your baby's to be any different.

You need to be gentle but you can still be firm. If you go slowly the baby will have a chance to yell if it's in pain before you do any serious damage (although if you go too slowly it may yell with boredom).

# THE PROCESS

1 **Assemble the clothes.** Before you begin, collect together all the clothes you want to put on the baby in one place. This should be somewhere safe and comfortable, which the baby can't roll off.

2 **Add the baby.** The other key ingredient for this exercise is the baby itself, so go and get it.

3 **Lie the baby down.** Lie it on its back. If you're putting a jumpsuit on it (that's one of those things that opens right down the front with poppers everywhere) open it up and lie the baby on top of it.

4 **Remove any existing clothing if necessary.** Unless you're simply adding an extra warm top or coat ready to go out, you'll need to take off any clothes the baby is wearing.

Undo all poppers, zips and ties first. Then put one hand inside the clothing and wriggle it down one of the sleeves or legs. When you reach the end, catch hold of the extremity you find there – hand or foot – and guide it back out of the sleeve or leg.

Repeat this with all necessary limbs until you have successfully freed the baby from its clothing. Once the legs and arms are released, slide the piece of clothing up to the neck (if it comes off that way) and then pull the front of it up over the head, preferably avoiding contact with the baby's face. If you try to pull clothes over the head from behind they may snag on the baby's chin. So always ease them over from the front. The baby should now be outside the clothes instead of the other way round.

5  **Change the baby's nappy** (optional). You've got this far, you might as well change its nappy while you're there unless you've just done so.

6  **Put the clothes on the baby.** The way you do this depends on what kind of clothing you're dealing with. Here are the techniques to use for the main types.

Always check how each article of clothing works before trying to use it.

○ **Clothes that go over the head.** Make the neck opening as wide as you can and slide it down over the baby's head, trying to avoid contact with the face as the baby probably won't like it. Put the baby's head gently down again; don't simply let it drop. Once the article of clothing has gone over the head, you need to get the baby's limbs into the thing.

The way to do this is to put your hand through the sleeve from the 'wrong' end (in other words the end the baby's hand will finally emerge through) and take hold of the baby's hand.

Then lead it gently back through the sleeve.

○ **Jumpsuit type things, coats and cardigans.** Lie the baby on top of the item of clothing and ease its legs and arms into the legs and sleeves as above. In the case of jumpsuits, get the baby into them feet first. Then do up the fastenings (or, in the case of those things with poppers everywhere, as many poppers as you can face doing).

○ **Trousers, shorts, and skirts.** Line up the baby with the item of clothing. Then put your hand in the 'wrong' end of the legs (or the bottom of the skirt) and take hold of the baby's foot (or both feet for a skirt). Ease it back out through the opening. You can gently lift the baby by its ankles until its bottom is raised up to pull the skirt or trousers up (be sure the baby is on its back for this procedure).

# Likely causes of crying

Hunger

Discomfort

Temperature

Wind

Nappy rash

Tiredness

# 12
# Stopping the baby crying

Babies cry. It's their thing. We shouldn't really begrudge them, after all it's the one skill they have which they can do better than us. You might find yourself wondering why they had to evolve to produce such a grating sound, when they could have made a noise like, say, a dove cooing or perhaps a cat purring instead. The answer of course is in the question: they have to make a seriously irritating noise, otherwise you might not get out of your warm bed in the middle of the night to do something about it.

**Core objective:** Stop the baby crying

**Key focus:** Make it happy again

Babies cry because something is wrong. All you have to do is find out what's wrong, and put it right. Then the baby will stop crying. OK, it's not always that simple but, surprisingly often, it is.

---

## Myth: you should never leave your baby to cry or you're traumatising it

As a general rule, there's no point in leaving your baby to cry. It's not likely to stop until you resolve its problem – it's hardly going to pull itself together and sort out its own problems at this stage – so if you ever want the noise to stop you'll have to do something and it might as well be now. On the whole, it's much better for the baby to get a prompt response so it knows you care. But there are times when you don't get to the baby as quickly as usual. Maybe you've just answered a vital phone call (which woke the baby) or perhaps you've spilt a bottle of red wine all over your white carpet. Don't panic: the baby will not suffer lifelong psychological damage if you leave it hungry or tired for a few minutes once in a while, and you're not a bad parent for doing it.

---

# THE PROCESS

When the baby cries, the only way to stop it is by finding out why it's crying and then responding to the need. When you have a small bundle of yelling baby in front of you, and no previous experience, finding out why it's crying can seem like trying to find a small piece of white paper somewhere in the Antarctic. But actually, it's simpler than you might think because there are really only three reasons why a small baby cries. Yep, it's that easy. Just run through the three reasons and you'll find the answer. So what are they?

## Hunger

All babies cry when they're hungry, and, speaking personally, I can really get behind that. Being hungry is a miserable state, and there's nothing wrong with any baby who has the sense to make the fuss it deserves. Too many of us have grown up to be polite and well mannered, but don't you just hate being kept waiting for food? I think we could all take a lead from our babies and start yelling about it.

If the baby is hungry, feed it. If you think it might be hungry, try feeding it. If this was the reason for the crying, your problem is solved.

## Discomfort

There are certain things which may make a baby uncomfortable and which you can check for to see if they are the cause of the crying. In particular, check for:

- Wind (see chaper 6).

- Nappy rash (see chapter 9).

- Temperature. Although babies will put up with a reasonable range of temperatures, they will complain if they are significantly too hot or too cold. So check this isn't the case.

If you think there is a chance the baby may be ill, or if its cry is recognisably different and more pained than usual, seek medical advice.

# Tiredness

Why babies can't just go to sleep when they're tired instead of making a big deal out of it isn't always entirely clear (but see page 122).

However, moany crying is often a sign of tiredness and if it's getting near nap time there's a good chance the baby needs to sleep.

Other clues, like yawning, can help indicate tiredness as the cause (that's the baby yawning, not you. You yawning is entirely normal and can happen at any time when you have a small baby).

The baby may have got it into its head that it won't go to sleep unless it's in one of its sleeping places. This may be its crib, the car seat, your arms or wherever it has grown used to sleeping in the short time since it was born. So put it in one of its sleeping spots and give it a chance to go to sleep.

# A fourth reason

Actually, if I'm honest, there's a fourth reason: bloody-mindedness. I'm sure child experts will tell you this is never the reason, and they're probably right, but there are times when this is the only reason you can find. It's unusual for a baby who is not tired, hungry or in pain to cry, but it does happen. Here are a few ideas for placating it:

- Cuddle it and soothe it.

- Give it a comforter (that's the proper word for a dummy) if you hold with them. Incidentally, if you're not sure about getting into the dummy habit, it's easy to wean a baby off them so long as you do it before they're about six months old. So you can use them for just the first few months. Dummies are also easier to wean a baby off than thumb sucking.

● Rock it gently.

● Sing to it or play music.

● Put it in the car and drive it around.

● Take it outside – just standing on the front door step will calm a lot of babies (although this is not recommended during blizzards, monsoons, electric storms or inside the Arctic circle).

As the baby gets older, it will think up new reasons to cry. After the first few weeks, for example, it may cry because it's bored or simply wants some company. A little later on frustration can cause it to cry – being unable to reach something for instance. However, by this time your experience will have caught up with the baby's and identifying the problem will seem less daunting. Sheer bloody mindedness will occasionally still be the cause, but you'll become more adept than you can imagine at detecting slight differences in the cry which indicates the problem. Half way into the first yell you'll be saying with confidence, 'Ah, he's dropped his rattle. Mmm, yes... to judge by the cry I'd say it's gone over the left side of the crib'.

Just a word of warning. Don't attempt to practise this newfound skill on anyone else's baby. The way other people's babies cry will continue to be as much of a mystery as it ever was.

# CRISIS MANAGEMENT

Sometimes a baby just yells and yells. Maybe it's got stubborn wind, or perhaps it's colicky. Maybe it's just constantly hungry. Whatever the reason, it is possible to get to the point when you start to lose control and you're frightened you'll actually hurt the baby just to make it shut up. Some babies hardly ever do this, but some poor parents have babies that seem to cry constantly. What do you do?

- The first thing is to recognise that you're not alone. Almost all parents have at least occasional moments when they feel like this. It doesn't make you a bad parent, it makes you a normal one.

The next thing to do is get away from the noise. Put the baby down on its back somewhere safe such as in its cot. Now leave it. Go into another room and scream, sob or whatever you need to do.

- Try to get a break. If you have a relative, friend or neighbour who will mind the baby for you while you go out – or simply go back to bed – this is the time to call in favours.

- Talk to your health visitor – this is part of their job.

- Call a helpline if you need to, especially if you're on your own and have no one to give you a break. The NSPCC have a helpline you can call (0808 800 5000), or you can ring the Samaritans (08457 90 90 90). It's what they're there for.

# Where will the baby sleep?

# 13

# Where to put the baby to sleep

There's a bewildering array of equipment designed for putting a baby in when it's time to go to sleep. And even when you've decided what to put it in, you still have to decide which room to use.

**Core objective:** Help the baby to go to sleep

**Key focus:** Keep it safe

The fact is that over the centuries, babies have somehow miraculously survived without baby baskets, cribs, cots, carrycots, prams and all the rest of it. These things are not, contrary to belief, essentials. They can make life easier – and you'll probably choose to get something to put the baby in – but you don't have to. Equally, if you go away overnight and forget to take the travel cot or whatever it is you use, the baby will come to no harm (and probably won't even care).

---

## Myth: you should put the baby in a proper crib or cot of some kind

I know babies who have been raised successfully sleeping in a drawer (not shut) or even a box (no lid, obviously). Once the baby can sit up and move about these options become more limited, but while it's tiny they do perfectly well. You can even (shock, horror) put your baby to sleep on the floor.

---

# WHAT DO YOU NEED?

This depends on the kind of routines you're planning. It's a bit of a catch-22 really. You don't know until you get there what you'll want, and by the time it happens your system will be dictated largely by the equipment you've already acquired. But here are a few points to think about:

- **Daytime sleeping.** Babies sleep in the daytime as well as at night. Many babies spend over half their time asleep (you can see why new fathers sometimes get jealous. It's nothing to do with attention; it's the sleep). You might decide that you would like the baby to nap during the day in the same place it sleeps at night, such as its bedroom cot. If this is the case you probably don't need a carrycot or Moses basket. However, if you want to let it sleep in the kitchen or living room where you can keep an eye on it, you may want a portable sleeping container of some kind.

- **Night-time sleeping.** Sooner or later you'll need some kind of cot – in other words a bed which the baby can't escape from or fall out of once it becomes mobile. So you can simply use this from the start. Some people use a smaller crib or cradle of some kind to begin with and then progress to a cot – quite unnecessary but they obviously get something out of it.

- **Sleeping out and about.** If you plan to take your baby out for walks on which you intend it to fall asleep, you'll want a pram or pushchair for the purpose. It will generally fall asleep in the car whether you want it to or not, and a car seat is compulsory anyway if your baby is going to travel in cars.

You can buy some pretty scary travel systems these days, which convert from car seats into prams into pushchairs into goodness knows what. I bet there's something out there that mixes up the milk and heats the bottle for you too, if you could ever decipher the instructions and work out which button to press. If this kind of thing overwhelms you, I advise you to steer clear of such systems. However, if you're good with mechanical things you can check them out.

Don't buy anything without getting a shop assistant to demonstrate it first, just to be sure it is actually possible to turn it inside out as the instructions imply.

These systems are pricey, but many parents say they are excellent. If you're fairly sure you're going to use all the variations it's probably worth the price. If you'd only use one or two configurations it's probably better to stick with the old-fashioned version.

# THE OPTIONS

I'm not going to list all the individual options and discuss each one. It seems more helpful to consider what criteria you should take into account when choosing which of the many pieces of equipment to buy (if any). Here are the main factors, not all of which will necessarily apply to you or your baby:

## Weight

If you are going to move the thing around, especially with the baby in it, you want it to be as light as possible. Suppose you put the baby in it to sleep downstairs after its feed, you might want to carry it upstairs where it can sleep undisturbed. For the first few days or even weeks, the mother is not going to be at her strongest and fittest.

## Portability

Some very lightweight pieces of sleeping equipment are still a sod to carry around. The handles are too short, the thing is too bulky to carry up stairs easily, it has a sharp metal corner that keeps getting you in the side of the leg... that sort of thing.

## Ease of travel

As well as carrying the thing around the house, you may also want to take it with you when you go away. Does it fold up? Or can you travel the baby in it, like a car seat? If the baby always sleeps in a cot at home, you may need only a car seat as well without investing in carrycots, cribs and so on.

## Feeling of being enclosed

The baby has spent the last few months snuggled up in warm near-darkness. The chances are that it will feel much cosier in something with high sides or a curtain round it than it will sleeping on a tray, for instance. Most baby sleeping gear is designed with this in mind.

## Price

Hmmm... big factor. This varies from nothing at all if you have generous friends who have just finished having their family, to hundreds of pounds. It's worth thinking through exactly what combination of equipment you want before you start buying, and price up in advance. A catalogue from one of the big baby retailers will give you a ballpark figure for the different types of equipment.

# YOUR BED OR THEIRS?

The question of whether or not you should have the baby in bed with you is hotly debated. There is some research that shows that the risk of SIDS (Sudden Infant Death Syndrome, or 'cot death') is up to 40 times greater if the baby shares your bed than if it sleeps in its own cot. Other evidence, however, suggests that so long as you fit certain conditions, it is safe to co-sleep (as it's known), and can even have benefits in terms of allowing the baby to moderate its breathing to your own. So what are these conditions? Well, it certainly isn't safe to co-sleep with the baby if you or your partner:

- Smokes
- Have been drinking
- Are obese
- Have been taking drugs
- Have a sleep disorder

You should also ensure that:

- The mattress is firm
- Any bedding is light
- The baby doesn't sleep on or near a pillow
- The baby can't become covered by the blanket or quilt
- The baby doesn't overheat
- The baby isn't left alone on the bed

If you can make sure all these conditions are in place, many experts agree that co-sleeping is a safe option. In the end, however, it's your baby and your choice.

Incidentally, there is agreement among experts that you should not sleep with your baby on a sofa or a waterbed (should you have one).

Here are the main pros and cons for sharing the bed with the baby:

| Pros | Cons |
|---|---|
| Babies who share a bed with their mothers cry less. | The baby may find it harder to get to sleep without you there. |
| You hardly have to wake up for a night time feed if you breastfeed. | You will be more disturbed generally through the night, although the disturbances will be more minor. |
| If you breastfeed, the baby will feed more in the night. You might question why this is a good thing. Well, night time milk, believe it or not, is even better for your baby than daytime milk. And the evidence is that you'll still get just as much sleep. | It can be difficult training the baby to sleep in its own bed later – such as when the next baby comes along. Are you sure you want to be sharing your bed with a five year old? |
| You'll be reassured that your baby is safe and well if it's right beside you. | Let's face it, a small baby in the bed does nothing for the spontaneity of your sex life (not that a small baby out of the bed does a great deal for it either...). |
| Both parents will feel close to the baby if they share a bed with it. | Bed sharing is particularly not recommended if either of you smokes, is on any drugs, has been drinking or suffers from sleep apnoea or a similar sleep disorder. These increase the risk of 'cot' death, or of lying on top of the baby and suffocating it. |

You can, of course, put the baby in its own room. You can buy an array of monitors to check its heart rate, monitor its breathing and amplify any sounds it makes. Or you can use the old-fashioned combination of a) listening, and b) checking on it from time to time. Since a major concern for all parents is cot death, it's worth pointing out that research shows that the risk of SIDS is reduced if you have the baby's cot in your room with you for the first six months.

An ideal solution is to put the baby right next to your bed where you can reach it, but still in its own cot or crib.

In view of the latest research, this would seem to be a far safer option than sharing your bed with the baby, or putting it in its own room. It also has the added advantage that it will become used to its own cot and will be less affected by moving to its own bedroom later since the cot will go with it.

If the baby sleeps in a cot remember to use what is called the 'feet to foot' position. In other words the baby's feet should be at the foot end of the cot, with any bedding only coming up to the baby's neck, so it can't wriggle down under the covers.

# What the baby needs to go to sleep

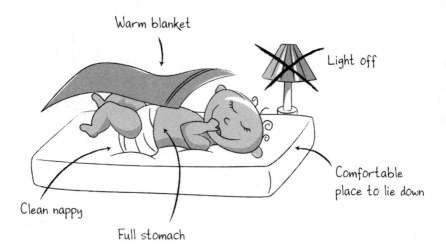

# 14

# Getting the baby to go to sleep

How do you get a baby to sleep? That's the $64 million question for most parents. You clearly can't get a baby to go to sleep when it's very hungry, or when it's in pain from wind, but you'd have thought that when it's warm, comfortable and well fed it would want to go to sleep. Well, maybe it does and maybe it doesn't. But either way, it may need your help.

**Core objective:** Getting the baby to go to sleep

**Key focus:** Have a healthy, well rested baby

There are times when wishful thinking takes over. Just because you want to sleep, you may be tempted to try to force a wakeful baby to sleep, kidding yourself that it must be as tired as you. This simply won't work, and can be extremely frustrating. Better to cut your losses and learn to recognise when the baby is and isn't tired. If it's clearly wide awake, abandon all hope of sleep. You'll feel a lot less frustrated that way.

---

## Myth: a healthy baby ought to sleep through the night with just one feed

Yep, lots of healthy babies do. And lots don't. Some babies will sleep through the night with no feed at all from day one. Others won't fall asleep in the first place until the early hours, and may be awake to feed again within a couple of hours. And a feed – often quoted as taking 'about an hour' – can take up to four hours for some babies. There is no standard model, and healthy babies know nothing about what they 'ought' to do. They just do what they need to do.

---

# A GOOD NIGHT'S SLEEP

Almost every parent can (and will) tell you dreadful stories about sleep deprivation in the first few weeks of a new baby's life. That's the parent, not the baby – who somehow always seems to get enough sleep even when you don't. A few lucky parents have sleep-through-the-night models, but these are rare. And even then if you ask what they mean they'll tell you their baby slept from 10pm to 6am. Well, I'm sorry, but waking at 6am doesn't constitute a good night's sleep in my book.

I'm in two minds what to say here. I don't want to be negative and leave you dreading those first few weeks. Nor do I want to lie to you and tell you it's all wonderful (plenty of people do and it makes you feel very alone when your baby never seems to sleep). So here are both sides of the picture.

## Positives

- You might be lucky and get a good sleeper. Of course, all babies have to sleep a lot, the trick is to catch them at it and join in. The ideal version is the type which sleeps a lot at night.

- Your body will learn to adapt quite quickly to a different sleep pattern so long as you still get enough sleep. Sleep when the baby sleeps, even during the day (you won't be able to do this with subsequent babies if you have an older child to look after, so make the most of it this time).

Don't be tempted to use the baby's nap time to catch up on chores. Abandon the chores and catch up on sleep instead.

You should notice a big improvement at around six weeks, when the baby starts to differentiate between night and day, and sleeps more at night. By three months you should notice another big improvement. Weaning onto solid food will again probably help the baby to sleep longer at night.

- Women have hormones which kick in around pregnancy and childbirth which help you cope better with sleep deprivation.

Breastfeeding will prolong production of these hormones. (Not much consolation there for fathers I'm afraid.)

● If you bottle feed the baby both parents can take turns at waking in the night to do the feed. Also, bottle fed babies tend to sleep longer at night because formula milk is more filling.

# Negatives

There's no denying that the worst scenario is pretty bad for a few weeks. Your baby may not sleep at all at night for the first few nights, and then start falling asleep for the first time at 3am or 4am.

● If you have a baby who sleeps badly or wakes a lot at night, you will find yourself, sooner or later, sobbing uncontrollably with exhaustion at four in the morning. This is perfectly normal. Most of us do it at some time; so ask for practical help if you possibly can, or at least emotional support. Other parents will understand (just steer clear of the ones who claim their baby 'slept right through from the start'. Who wants to hang out with people like that?).

● The really tough stretch – the first six weeks – lasts longer than most paternity leave which can make sharing the burden tricky. If you breastfeed the baby you can't share the night time feeds with your partner.

If you feel you really are reaching the end of your tether – and along with a crying baby, sleep deprivation is the most likely thing to cause this – take action before you hurt the baby. Put the baby somewhere safe such as its cot and leave the room. It will probably yell, but it won't come to any serious harm. Sit in another room for as long as you need to feel you can cope when you return. Call someone for help; during hours you can call your health visitor. Otherwise, if you don't know anyone personally who you can call, there's always the NSPCC helpline, NHS Direct or the Samaritans (all in the phone book).

# KNOWING WHEN IT'S TIME FOR SLEEP

You'll learn to recognise the signs pretty quickly. Babies traditionally sleep after a good meal (a habit which lasts throughout life, given the chance). So if the baby's just had a good feed it's a fair bet it might fancy a kip. There are other telltale signs too, such as yawning or rolling its eyes upwards (no, it's not auditioning for a horror movie, it just looks as if it is).

To give the baby the best chance of going to sleep, make sure it has a clean nappy and is comfortable and warm (but not too warm). You can change the nappy and get the baby ready towards the end of a feed. It won't thank you for changing its nappy at the start of the feed when it's hungry (in fact, it won't thank you for much, quite frankly, for several years, if then). However, leaving the change until it's falling asleep will just wake it up again. So change its nappy once the hunger is sated but before it has quite finished feeding. Kind of between main course and pudding.

Some babies enjoy being swaddled for the first few weeks, if you do this from the start. This entails wrapping them up in a sheet so they feel secure (because it's a bit like being in the womb). It can encourage the baby to sleep peacefully.

If you want to try this, ask your midwife to demonstrate how it's done.

# SETTING PATTERNS

The most useful thing you can do for both you and the baby is to get it into a falling asleep routine as quickly as possible. The principle is quite simple. We all find it easier to get to sleep if we follow some kind of ritual. You probably like to plump your pillow first, or lie in a particular position, or have the covers right up to your neck, or recite the alphabet under your breath, or some other personal ritual for falling asleep.

Well, babies are just the same. Only you have a blank canvas to work with for the first couple of days (it won't take long to establish a ritual). What you need to do is to give your baby a consistent routine for falling asleep. This might involve being rocked, being sung or played music to, having a piece of cloth which smells of its mother, having the lights at a particular level, being stroked or whatever.

The thing is, whatever pattern you set, it will be very hard to change without a lot of resistance (i.e. yelling) from the baby.

So you need to establish a pattern which is safe and comforting for the baby, but which is also convenient for you. If your baby learns to fall asleep being rocked, you could be stuck rocking it for hours. This may not bother you – especially if you have, say, a swinging crib. On the other hand, it might drive you to tears at three o'clock in the morning when you've been rocking it for an hour and every time you stop it wakes up and yells.

If the baby is going to sleep in your bed, having it fall asleep in your arms at the end of a feed probably won't matter. But if it's not in bed with you, and it then won't stand for being transferred to its cot, falling asleep in your arms may be a big issue.

Broadly speaking, if you want the baby to sleep on its own – even if it's right next to the bed – you'd do well to set a sleep pattern right from the start which involves the baby falling asleep lying in its cot or Moses basket. You can stroke it softly, which is much easier to stop without waking it than rocking it in your arms.

Ah but you may be thinking, what if it falls asleep in your arms while you're feeding it? In that case, if you want it to be able to fall asleep on its own, simply move it once it's asleep and, if it wakes, let it learn to settle back to sleep by itself. If you do this right from the start it should settle into the routine very happily. And remember, whatever pattern you set, you need to follow it for daytime as well as night time sleeping. The baby won't differentiate between the two for several weeks.

You may think this sounds cold and heartless. If your chosen routine involves shutting it in a rat-infested dungeon until it learns to like it, I'd agree with you. But if it involves lying the baby in a comfortable, familiar cot, with low lighting and a piece of cloth that smells of its mother (if you're breastfeeding keep the cloth in your bra), while you sing and stroke it gently until it falls asleep, I can't see a problem with it.

In fact, you're doing the baby a big favour. The easier it is for the baby to go to sleep, the better rested it will be. And so will you. I fell into the trap myself with my first baby. I found that he wouldn't fall asleep unless I swung him to and fro in his Moses basket for up to 45 minutes (if I stopped swinging, he woke up). I don't know how the habit started, but the baby got swung to sleep during the day and before long I found myself having to swing him in the middle of the night. Being a 10lb baby he fed several times a night, and was extremely heavy to swing each time - especially given that I hadn't fully recovered from the birth. With my subsequent babies we made sure we set a pattern which was warm and comforting for the baby, and manageable for us too.

# STAYING ASLEEP

Just because you got the baby to go to sleep, that doesn't mean it's going to stay asleep.

Oh, no. Babies aren't that uncomplicated. No baby is going to stay asleep through hunger, poohing, pain or excessive cold. But even if you've eliminated all these factors, the baby may still wake before you want it to. Here are the most common reasons for this.

## Noise

Many babies will sleep through any amount of noise, so don't assume you have to tiptoe round, hushing everyone and cursing in whispers whenever the phone rings. That's no kind of a life for anyone. So try making a noise and see if you can get away with it. Then again, some babies genuinely are light sleepers.

Lots of people say that babies that are used to noise – especially those with older siblings – will sleep through anything. Some will, but I've known babies way down the family who wake if a pin drops.

If the baby is a really light sleeper, it's better to let it sleep well away from the hubbub of family life rather than try to make the entire household act like pantomime robbers tiptoeing exaggeratedly and shushing each other.

## Movement

Here's a classic. The baby goes to sleep in your arms beautifully. You know it's tired and you're feeling proud of your success getting it to drop off to sleep. Now all you need to do is lie it down in its cot. You manage, with difficulty and no dignity whatsoever, to manoeuvre yourself into a standing position. You set off towards the cot, creeping silently and somehow managing to keep your arms locked in exactly the same position throughout.

You reach the cot, and gently lower the baby into it, a fraction of an inch at a time, as if it were some archeological treasure being slowly craned into position. You finally ease the baby onto the mattress, slide your arms out bit by bit from under it, stand up, and breathe a sigh of relief.

The baby opens its eyes suddenly and yells. Ha! It's been waiting! You know it has! It was awake all along and just winding you up. Barely a few days old and already it has a sense of humour and it's practising it on you.

I have no idea why babies have to do this, but don't take it personally. It's not just your baby, it's all of them, if that makes you feel any better. There are three options. One is to start all over again (and let the baby wake up at the last minute all over again). The second is to leave the baby to cry itself to sleep. There are mixed views on whether this is a good thing, and you probably have your own opinion on the matter. The third is to encourage the baby to fall asleep in its final sleeping location from the off. This neatly sidesteps the whole problem, and is what setting sleeping patterns is all about.

## Stopping the car

If the baby has fallen asleep in the car, turning off the engine may wake it up. There's not a lot you can do about this, except view the sleep in the car as a bonus, rather than the waking up as a frustration. Or keep driving round until the baby wakes (try not to think about the eco-guilt, as the longer the baby sleeps the worse damage you do to the world it will grow up in). Many babies, however, will stay asleep as long as you leave them alone. In this case, aim to leave the baby in the car seat and take the whole shebang out of the car. If you're arriving home, bring the car seat indoors and let the baby go on napping in it. If you're out and about, this is where one of those combination things that turns from a car seat into a pushchair is so handy.

## Wind

This is incredibly frustrating, be warned. The baby is just ready to fall asleep, but it's too uncomfortable because it has wind so it starts crying instead.

By the time you've dealt with the wind, the baby's wide awake again. Console yourself with the knowledge that it will probably sleep better when it finally gets to sleep. Although the baby seems wide awake and ready to be entertained for the next couple of hours, it is quite capable of being sound asleep again in five minutes. The wind issue doesn't actually delay things for as long as you think it will, and it has to be dealt with. Almost always. Just occasionally, the baby clearly has wind but seems quite happy to sleep through it. Let it. It's the baby's call. If the discomfort gets too great the baby will let you know, don't worry.

# Habit

Babies can get into the habit of waking, especially in the night. In fact, all babies wake frequently and then settle back to sleep almost immediately. But if they cry for a moment or two, it's easy to fall into the habit of comforting them back to sleep. This can become habit in the space of a night or two, and the baby then can't get back to sleep without your presence, rocking, stroking or whatever it is that has become the getting back to sleep pattern. Both you and the baby then suffer from disturbed sleep, and the baby is worse off than if you ignored the brief crying. So ignore it.

A very small baby is probably crying because it needs a feed, which is a different matter altogether and of course you should feed it.

And I'm not suggesting you should ignore prolonged crying or any sign of pain or discomfort. But you need to be on the lookout for setting a pattern of waking for no particular reason and then being unable to settle without help from a parent. It commonly starts if the baby is genuinely disturbed through the night by something like a cold and a blocked nose.

For a couple of nights you go to it when it wakes distressed and then, before you know it, the baby is fully recovered but you're still going to comfort it 15 or 20 times a night.

If this happens – and it can happen to the best of us – the best solution is generally to be cruel to be kind. Ignore the cries for a night or two and the old getting back to sleep routine will be re-established within days. This sounds very straightforward and, from a practical point of view, it is. Emotionally, however, it can be very distressing. You may well find yourself far more upset than the baby.

But remind yourself that everyone is better off sleeping happily – the baby included – and it should take less than a week to get back to normal.

# Walking the baby: things to prepare for

Make sure the baby won't get wet if it rains

Make sure the baby won't be too hot or too cold

Check if the baby is due a feed soon. If so, take the milk with you

Change the nappy before you go, and take a spare if you're going to be gone long

# 15
# Taking the baby for a walk

Why would you want to take the baby for a walk? Well, quite possibly because you need to go for a walk – to the post office, the shops, to visit a friend – and you can't very well leave the baby behind. However, variety and stimulation are also good for the baby; they help it to develop and to stay happy. Also, a walk often helps the baby go to sleep when it's clearly time for a nap but the baby doesn't seem to want to cooperate.

**Core objective:** Go for a walk, taking the baby along too

**Key focus:** Bring the baby back safely

Fresh air is great for the baby (should you be lucky enough to have any of the stuff round where you live) and it certainly stimulates their senses. Curiously, as well as stimulating the baby, fresh air will also send it to sleep. So rather than feel stuck at home with the baby, a walk – even a short one – will make both of you feel better. And it will give you an opportunity to start learning how that pushchair/pram/ combination thingy folds up and re-opens.

---

## Myth: you should take the baby out for a walk every day

There's no harm in doing this at all, but it certainly isn't compulsory. Your mother or grandmother may tell you that's what they did, but actually that's only because they had nothing else to do with the baby and probably had no car.

---

# THE PROCESS

1  **Change the baby's nappy** (see chapter 8). If you don't do this before you go out, sod's law will operate and you'll regret your lack of forethought.

2  **Fetch the pushchair/pram/combination thingy.** If you have the baby in your arms before you do this, you'll be trying to unfold it one-handed, when we all know it's virtually impossible even with the full quota of hands. This is a standard approach with almost all baby-related activities, actually. Introducing the baby into the equation should almost always be the final stage. It will only get in the way otherwise.

3 **Open the pushchair/pram/combination thingy.** No this isn't a joke. You know everyone always told you that being a parent is a steep learning curve? Well, operating the baby is nothing. It's operating all the equipment which is the steepest part of the curve. Don't ever attempt to do this with anyone else, especially your partner, as it can lead to serious rows.

4 **Consider the relative indoor/outdoor temperatures.** You don't want the baby to overheat, but you don't want it to freeze either. In high summer you may not need to put any extra clothes on the baby, but most of the year it will need at least a little extra something to go out, especially if your house is centrally heated. Bear in mind that the baby isn't any more sensitive to the cold than you are, but unlike you it won't be moving about to warm itself up. So put another layer of clothing on the baby before you put it in the pushchair/ pram/combination thingy.

5 **Put the baby in the pushchair/pram/combination thingy safely.** It really is important to do the right straps up in the right way, to be sure the baby doesn't fall out or get tangled up in the inner workings of the pushchair. If you go over bumps, or break into a sprint to escape someone you've just spotted across the road, you need to know that the baby can't come to any harm.

6 **Add a blanket if you need to.** With enough clothes this won't be necessary, but if you're not sure about the outside temperature, it's easier to add a light layer of clothing and a blanket which you can remove, rather than a thick layer of clothing which is a pain to take off the baby in transit.

7 **Take a raincover.** Don't assume that it won't rain if it's looking iffy, or you're asking for trouble. Having said that,

I've brought up three babies and never owned a raincover; they're not essential. The alternative is not taking the baby out if it looks like rain or, in an emergency, taking off your own coat to cover it with while you get soaked and frozen. Well, it's your own fault for not buying a raincover (so I've been told many a time).

8  **Check the time.** If you go out for a half hour walk five minutes before the baby's next feed is due, you have only yourself to blame if it yells most of the way. So for your own sake as well as the baby's, don't stay out past feed time unless you've taken the feeding wherewithal with you.

When you get back from the walk, you can leave the baby in the pushchair/pram/ combination thingy if it's asleep, so long as you park it somewhere safe (such as in your hallway) and remove the blanket if you think it may overheat. When you take the baby out, put it down somewhere safe before attempting to fold the wretched thing up again. If you have the space, you should aim never to fold the pushchair/pram/combination thingy up.

Once opened, keep it open for evermore and be the envy of all the parents you know who don't have as much room as you.

# In-car checklist
Keep these items permanently in the car so you can't forget them

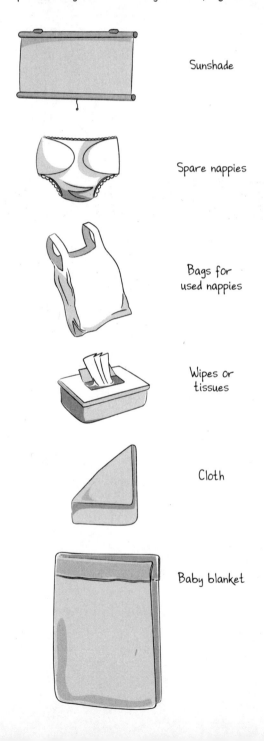

Sunshade

Spare nappies

Bags for
used nappies

Wipes or
tissues

Cloth

Baby blanket

# 16

# Taking the baby in the car

Unless the baby's world is to be restricted to a few miles from the house, you're going to want to put it in a car sooner or later. Once you get used to it, taking the baby in the car needn't be a palaver at all. What's more, it can be a great way to get it to go to sleep.

**Core objective:** Travel from A to B by car with the baby

**Key focus:** Get the baby there and back safely

Car seats are frequently a pain to fit into the car, whether they are of the permanent variety or the kind you lift in and out. This test of initiative/patience is part of what being a parent is all about. Once you can fit a car seat one-handed while holding a conversation and carrying the baby, you can remove the metaphorical L plates and consider yourself a proper parent.

---

## Myth: you don't need to bother with a car seat if you're just going a short distance; you can carry the baby on your lap

Oh no you can't. You'll be breaking the law and risking the baby's life. I know your mother says it's what she did with you and you never came to any harm, but plenty of babies sadly did. A car seat is essential even if you're only going half way round the block (in which case it would be far healthier to put the baby in a pushchair and walk anyway).

---

# CHOOSING A CAR SEAT

What you really want is a car seat that you can put a newborn baby into and then keep using until the child is about six years old and doesn't need a car seat any more. You'll find a dazzling array of car seats on offer, but nowhere among them will you find one that fits this description. What you will find, roughly speaking, is the following:

- Up to nine months of age or thereabouts, a baby is safest in a rear-facing car seat. Some of these convert into pushchair/pram/combination thingies, and some are simply plain old car seats. You're going to need one of some description if you'll ever be taking the baby out in a car.

- From nine months to four years, a child needs a forward facing seat. You're going to have to acquire another seat. At least this one can be counted on not to confuse you by trying to mutate into other pieces of equipment before your eyes. It's a car seat and that's that. It's known in the manufacturers' jargon as a 'second-stage' car seat.

- From four until about six years (it's really down to the child's height so it's around six years) the child will need a booster seat. Cushions aren't safe enough – you really do need a proper seat which has guides for the car seat belt. Either you now have to buy a third item, or you had the foresight at nine months to buy a second-stage seat which will convert into a booster seat later on (the back section separates from the seat in some way).

If you really want to get your money's worth out of all this equipment, your best bet is to have at least three children, preferably spaced around two years apart. Although, of course, you will find that this option carries other cost implications.

# THE PROCESS

To begin with, you'll have a rear-facing car seat, which will lift in and out of the car, so these instructions are for the first nine months until you upgrade to a car seat which may be permanently fitted. By then, you'll know what you're doing and you're on your own, mate.

1  **Collect together everything you need.** Unless your car is parked right outside the front door in a private driveway and, in earshot while you're in the house, you don't want to leave the baby alone in it while you nip back indoors and collect the shopping list, find your keys, find your purse, lock the back door, answer the phone, make up a bottle to take with you, leave a note for your partner... and anything else that comes to mind. So do all those things while the baby is in the house with you. Then you can both head for the car together, shutting the front door behind you as you go.

2  **Get the baby ready.** Change its nappy, put on any extra clothes, and anything else you think might be necessary.

3  **Put the baby in the car seat and strap it in.** You'll have to follow the manufacturer's instructions here. The important thing is not to forget to strap the baby in safely.

4  **Put the car seat in the car and strap it in.** More strapping. Not only must the baby be firmly attached to the car seat, but the car seat must be firmly attached to the car. Double check that everything is connected up properly, with no twists in seat belts and so on. One of the biggest dangers arises when you leave the car seat in the car - for example you take the baby out of it to put it into its pushchair (if you don't have one of those car seat/pushchair/pram combination thingies). When you replace the baby, you strap the baby to the seat and, sensing unconsciously that you've done the strapping in thing, you then forget to strap the seat to the car. If you have the kind of car seat arrangement where this is possible, get into the habit (as quickly as possible) of checking both sets of straps before you drive off.

# Keep it in the car

There are certain pieces of equipment it is handy to keep in the car permanently. That way, you have less to remember each time you go out. Here's a short list of things you might want to stock your car with:

- A sunshade for the window next to the baby's seat
- Spare nappies, and bags to put the used ones in
- Baby wipes or tissues
- Muslin cloth or some kind of cloth for cleaning up spills, baby sick etc
- Baby blanket

Once the baby is about three months old, you may want to have two or three small baby toys to keep it amused, or maybe one of those soft bars that fixes across the baby seat and has toys dangling from it.

# How to play with the baby

Talk to it

Show it things

Sing to it

Spin it slowly

# 17

# Playing with the baby

Babies spend most of their time sleeping or feeding. However there are gaps in between these activities, during which you may feel it incumbent on you to interact with the baby in some way. But how?

**Core objective:** Stimulate the baby

**Key focus:** Don't injure it

Play is just another word for learning to a small child. To be more precise, it means learning while having fun. Babies can't help learning; it's what they're built for. So long as they're stimulated, they're learning. So playing with the baby just means stimulating it – its brain and its five senses.

## Myth: there's no point talking to a baby; it won't understand what you're saying

Actually, if you don't speak to it when it's small, it will never understand a word you're saying. It may take a baby a couple of years or so to master speech, but it starts the process of learning it even before it's born. You can't talk to your baby too much.

Some people naturally fall into easy conversation with newborns, apparently oblivious to the fact that the baby barely understands them. Since it won't argue, answer back, interrupt or wander off, you can see why many people find them such rewarding companions. However, others of us haven't a clue how to interact with a new baby, even when it's our own. It takes only a few weeks to get comfortably into the habit, but you may like some ideas to kick you off.

# TALKING

Talking to the baby is the most stimulating way to interact with it at this age. After all, you can't yet kick a football around with it, or teach it to play Monopoly, but you can talk to it. It's worth emphasising that research shows that talking in the same room as a baby, or putting it in front of a radio or TV, or chatting with someone else in front of it, teach it almost nothing about language. It needs you to talk directly to it, making eye contact. Here are some pointers:

- Babies respond best to the style of talking known as 'motherese', which is instinctive to many parents. It's that way of talking in a high voice, smiling a lot, over emphasising key words, and using a sing-song pattern of speech. Just imagine you're talking to a very stupid person who doesn't speak your language, and you've just about got it.

- While motherese sing-song is great for babies, it doesn't help to talk in baby language, as in 'goo-goo diddums, ickle babbykins' and that kind of garbage. Babies may be ignorant but they're not stupid, and they don't want to listen to that any more than you do.

Babies love repetition. You can say the same thing several times and it will help them to learn it. In fact, even after you've said the same thing a dozen times, they still won't accuse you of nagging or wittering. They'll appreciate it. This is why many children's rhymes and stories are repetitive.

- Why not sing to the baby? You can sing children's songs (you're going to have to brush up on them sooner or later) or your own personal favourites. The baby will particularly appreciate those which have actions. Whatever you sing, just make sure you sing it to the baby, not simply to yourself as you go about your chores, if you want to interact with it.

- Babies like rhymes which they can get to recognise. Things like 'Round and round the garden like a teddy bear' or 'Incy wincy spider' (running your fingers up the baby's tummy as the spider comes out of the water spout) appeal on several levels: the baby learns to recognise the words, to enjoy the physical sensations, and to anticipate the actions.

- Nappy changing time is a good time for interactive games and talking, from a ritual 'Uh, oh! What's in the nappy?' or 'Pop! Pop! Pop!' as you do up the poppers on its clothes, to more complex games.

Many babies come to love nappy changing time if you do this, and really enjoy the one-to-one attention they get.

- If you're stuck for something to say to the baby, you can always give it a running commentary on what you're up to. So long as you engage with it rather than talk over it, it will be happy listening to you describe how you're hanging out the socks to dry, or opening the morning post. You'll never have such an appreciative audience again, so don't waste the opportunity.

- You may think you can't tell if the baby is getting anything out of this or not. For the first few weeks it won't even smile. But if its attention is on you, and it's trying to respond with eye contact, you know you're doing the right thing.

- Don't worry if you can only keep this kind of conversation going for a few minutes at a time. If you're alone with the baby for several hours a day, it's not feasible to keep talking to it constantly. Just do it as often as you can when the baby is awake and active.

# STIMULATING THE OTHER SENSES

Babies are fairly delicate objects, and you don't want to treat yours roughly. Nevertheless, there are plenty of ways to stimulate it physically which won't hurt it. Here are a few:

- The baby's sight still has a long way to go to be as good as yours, but it can make out shapes, and has better close-up than long-distance vision.

  You can carry your baby around the house and garden and show it things, bearing in mind that it will see strong shapes and contrasts best, especially those about 18 inches away from it.

- You can sing to it, or play it music, or sing along to a musical toy.

- It will be a few months before the baby can hold a toy and play with it by itself. In the meantime you can stimulate the baby's sense of touch by stroking its cheek with a fleece blanket or a clean feather, or something slightly colder or warmer than room temperature. Tell the baby what the object is as you do this.

- Babies love movement, and it helps to develop their sense of balance. It won't be long before you can start playing gentle tossing games with the baby, throwing it (carefully) up in the air (and catching it again) but wait until its neck is stronger before you start on this. In the meantime, babies love to be spun round, and it helps develop their sense of balance. If you have a swivel chair, you can sit on it holding the baby and gently spin the chair.

These are a few suggestions to get you started. Once you get used to playing with the baby you'll come up with lots of ideas of your own. So long as you remember your key focus – don't injure it – just about anything goes if it stimulates and entertains the baby.

## Do babies need toys?

A baby isn't really in a position to get much benefit from toys when it's very young. All those teddy bears and rattles you've been given will come into their own later, but don't be disappointed when the baby doesn't give them a second glance right now. The only toy that really appeals to it at this stage is you. You can walk and talk and respond to it and, within weeks, it will respond to you in turn.

If you can't afford lots of fancy toys, it really doesn't matter. Your grandparents and their forebears managed to grow up without them. Babies are a bit like kittens – happy for hours with nothing but a ball of string. (The only difference is that you should never give a baby a ball of string. OK, that's quite a big difference.) The point is that toys are only one way for a small child to learn about the world. A four-month-old baby will play as happily with a wooden spoon out of the kitchen drawer, or your hairbrush, as it will with most baby toys. So there's no need to regard an abundance of toys as an essential for the baby; they're simply an optional extra.

# Starting position for feeding baby solid food

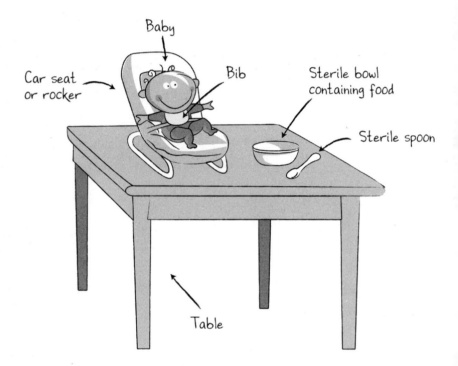

Baby

Car seat
or rocker

Bib

Sterile bowl
containing food

Sterile spoon

Table

# Weaning onto solid food

Sooner or later your baby's going to need something more substantial than milk to help it grow and stay healthy.

**Core objective:** Get the food down the baby

**Key focus:** Don't choke it

Current advice is to start introducing the baby to solid food between four and six months of age. You can do this very gradually, taking several weeks to build up to three solid meals a day – although some babies clearly want to go faster than this (don't worry, if you have one of these models you'll know). Nevertheless, the first few solid feeds are inevitably nerve-wracking to some extent.

Just remind yourself that every other parent feels the same way; you'll soon be shovelling food down the kid like an expert.

---

## Myth: babies should be started on solid food when they are four months old

Although this is a very common age to start on solid food, many babies don't start until later. The advice is not to start before four months, and not to leave it beyond six months. Anywhere in this range is fine, just go by what seems to suit your particular baby. If your baby was premature, or very large and hungry, you may feel that these guidelines aren't appropriate. You can always ask your doctor or health visitor for advice that is specific to your baby.

---

# WHEN IS THE BABY READY FOR SOLIDS?

Some babies are ready much sooner than others, and you'll be able to tell when yours gets to the right stage for solid food because there are useful telltale signals:

- You may notice the baby watching you eat, following the fork from your plate to your mouth. If it's this interested, it's probably keen to find out for itself what's going on.

- The baby may seem hungrier than usual by the time it's around four months. This is a clue that it's ready to try solids.

- Equally, the baby may demand more frequent milk feeds.

- When the time the baby spends asleep between feeds at night starts to decrease, so that it wakes more frequently for night feeds, that's a fairly clear sign that milk alone is no longer giving the baby the sustenance it used to, and a solid supplement would satisfy it better.

# WHAT FOOD SHOULD YOU GIVE?

You need to start your baby on the most basic foods and build from there. There are plenty of books which tell you about what to feed babies as they grow, so I'll just concentrate on the first few weeks. After that, you won't be a beginner any more.

The most important thing – your key focus – is to make sure the baby doesn't choke. The baby itself can look after the eating and swallowing process by instinct; your task is to make sure the food is sufficiently mushy and slushy that it contains no lumps.

Here are a few ideas for suitable first foods:

● Vegetable purées (eg potato, carrot, courgette, sweet potato, peas)

● Fruit purées (eg apple, pear, banana)

● Baby rice (which you can buy at the baby aisle in supermarkets)

There are some foods you should avoid for the first few months, either because they are difficult for a baby to digest, or because they may trigger allergies. The main foods or food groups to avoid are:

● Wheat-based foods (including bread)

● Dairy foods (including cow's milk)

● Eggs

● Citrus fruit

● Nuts

● Fatty foods

● Very spicy foods such as chillies

# Top tips for feeding

- If you introduce only one food at a time, you'll be able to tell easily if your baby doesn't like something or reacts badly to it.

- Just because the baby refused a certain food once, don't necessarily write it off. Maybe it was full up, or had wind, or was simply in a grouchy mood. So try the food again after a few days to see how adamant the baby really is.

- Don't add salt or sugar to the baby's food, and avoid pre-prepared foods which contain added salt or sugar.

- Bananas and avocados are both suitable from the early stages, and have a particular benefit: they come inside a sterile outer skin. Both of them have flesh which turns to mush when scraped with a spoon, so you can feed the baby directly from the fruit. This is particularly handy if you're out for the day since, as with jars of baby food, you don't need to worry about sterilising bowls and so on. Unlike jars, however, the food is completely fresh.

- Babies are only human, and they like variety. Give them a decent range of foods. Although you should avoid hot spices, you can try making foods more interesting by adding a small quantity of mild spices for flavour. You might add cinnamon to apple purée, for instance, or ground ginger to sweet potato purée.

- You can make up fruit and vegetable purées in bulk and freeze them in small portions.

- If your baby is frequently hungry, you can mix baby rice with fruit or vegetables to make it more substantial.

# WHAT TIME OF DAY SHOULD YOU GIVE THE FIRST FEED?

You can give a solid meal at any time of day you like – you won't do the baby any harm. However, you might like to consider these factors:

- At this age, milk is the most important food for the baby nutritionally, so it's best not to give a solid feed before a milk feed as this may spoil the baby's appetite for milk. Straight after a milk feed, or between feeds, is generally better.

- Since a solid meal will help the baby sleep, you might well want to start it off with an evening meal so that everyone gets a better night's sleep.

- Then again – especially if the baby is a good sleeper anyway – a lunchtime feed means that any minor stomach gripes as a result of the solid food won't interrupt everyone's sleep.

- It will help the baby's sleeping and feeding habits to build a routine.

Also, once it gets into the habit of being fed at a particular time, it will start feeling hungry around that time.

So although it will do the baby no harm to adjust its feed time just occasionally due to force of circumstance, the closer you can keep to a firm routine, the easier it will be for everyone. This continues to apply as you build up to three meals a day.

# THE PROCESS

1   **Sterilise the spoon, and the bowl if you're using one.** If you're feeding the baby from a sterile jar, or direct from the banana skin for example, you won't necessarily need a bowl, but any non-sterile equipment should be sterilised.

2   **Get the baby comfortable.** You can't feed it lying down, but it may be too young to sit up without help. If it's too young for a high chair you may be able to feed it in a baby rocker if you have one, in its rear-facing car seat (you don't have to go out to the car to do this) or on someone else's lap. You can feed it on your own lap, but you'll kind of miss having both hands free for feeding with. Best to graduate to this stage over a few days.

3   **Put a bib on the baby.** You'll need it, trust me. If you don't have a bib a cloth will do, but don't tie it round the baby's neck.

4   **Prepare the food.** This may simply mean taking the lid off the jar, or it might mean liquidising fruit or vegetables and putting them in a sterile bowl.

5   **Offer the baby a taste.** The baby isn't daft. It's going to want to taste this stuff before it opens its mouth wide for you to shovel it in. So give it a tiny taste of the end of the spoon and give it time to mull it over. It will almost certainly open its mouth for more.

6   **Give the baby a small spoonful.** Assuming the baby wants more, give it what it wants. Give it small spoonfuls, and allow it plenty of time to swallow each one before you offer it the next. Contrary to all your expectations the baby will, in fact,

not choke; mushy first foods are almost as much a drink as they are a food, and babies can manage them perfectly well.

7  **Keep feeding it for a bit.** When the baby opens its mouth for another spoonful, that's a surefire sign that it wants more. See – it's not difficult, this feeding lark.

8  **When the baby has had enough, stop.** It doesn't matter how little (or how much) your baby eats, so long as it has all the food it wants. If you have a very hungry baby it may want more than you'd expected; that's fine. One of mine demanded second helpings of his first ever meal, and went straight on to three large meals a day. My next ate only one modest meal a day for the first three weeks. So there's no right or wrong. However, if you try to get too much down a baby that really isn't up for it, it is more likely to cause wind and discomfort.

9  **Clean the baby up.** The older and more experienced the baby becomes, the messier it will get. I don't know why this should be – you'd have thought experience would make it tidier – but I guess it doesn't have the same priorities as you. This is a trend which continues until it reaches about 18 months or so.

10 **Tidy everything else up.** Off with the bib, wash and sterilise all the equipment, and give yourself a pat on the back. Your baby is now eating solid food.

# AFTER THE FIRST MEAL

Once the baby has finished its first meal, you may notice one or two irregular things. It's worth knowing what these are so that you don't worry about them:

- The baby may experience a bit of wind or farting over the next few hours. This is the digestive system's very first chance to practise with real food, and it will take it a while to get the hang of it.

- The baby may well sleep for much longer than usual at its next sleep. There's no need to panic and check constantly that it's still breathing (although please do if it helps you). This is quite normal.

- Its pooh will become more solid and may change colour once the baby starts eating solid food. The colour can vary according to what it's been eating lately.

# Feeding hiccups

If the baby refuses to eat the food, don't worry about it. If you suspect that it simply disliked the taste, try giving it something different. If you think it was averse to the whole idea of solid food, wait a few days and try again. Sooner or later it will eat – when it's ready. It's an instinct and it's bound to happen. If you're concerned about the baby not eating, especially once it reaches about six months old, have a word with your health visitor.

The baby's appetite will change. Sometimes it will eat ferociously, then for a few days it will seem to eat almost nothing. This is quite normal behaviour. The best way to judge if the baby is getting enough food is not by the amount it eats, but by its energy levels and general health. If you clearly have an energetic, happy, healthy child then don't worry. However, always see your health visitor if you want reassurance or are concerned that the baby isn't as lively as usual.

Sometimes, babies go through phases of moaning and griping when you feed them. Often this seems to be simply a phase you have to put up with – again, it's perfectly normal but do get professional advice if you're concerned. Some of the more everyday reasons for this, which you might like to consider, include:

● The baby wants to eat faster than you can feed it. This generally wears off part way through the meal as the worst of its hunger is sated. The baby is used to milk being supplied in a continuous flow, and it may not appreciate the constant interruptions to the flow of food. You'll have to choose whether to try and feed it faster, or whether to make it slow down even if it moans about it; there isn't a right and wrong way to deal with it.

- The baby wants to feed itself. Quite impractical at this age, but you can give it a spoon to hold (sterilised of course) which may keep it happy.

- It doesn't like the food you're giving it. You can't assume that just because it liked mashed carrot last week, it will necessarily like it this week. (You must have been there yourself.) You might want to try something different to see if this is the problem.

- The baby wants someone else to feed it. Yep, some babies are only happy if Daddy feeds them, or Mummy, especially if their preferred slave is in the room. Only you can decide whether to cooperate with this or not.

# Typical signs of teething

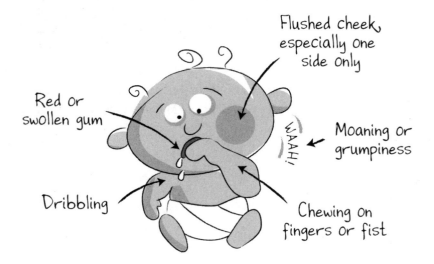

# 19

# Teething

Babies are born without teeth. Toddlers have teeth. Ergo, babies have to acquire teeth. This happens quite naturally as the teeth push through the gums, one at a time, sometime during the baby's first year or so. This process is painful to the baby, and the baby will let you know as much.

**Core objective:** Ease the baby's pain

**Key focus:** The same

There is a limit to how much you can do to ease the pain of teething, unfortunately, and you need to resign yourself to the fact that the baby's gums are going to hurt and you're not going to be able to stop it. Comfort yourself with the knowledge that the baby has to learn to get used to pain sooner or later and teething, while unpleasant for a small baby with a low pain threshold, really isn't dangerous or serious. I don't mean to be callous at all – it's not pleasant to watch your own baby in pain – but it will help you to keep it in proportion and respond with mild concern rather than serious worry.

---

## Myth: diarrhoea, sickness and nappy rash are generally signs of teething

Many doctors will tell you this is nonsense, and as many parents and grandparents will tell you it's true. The fact is that no one is certain and these symptoms may sometimes be linked to teething. What is important, however, is not to assume that teething is the cause, and consequently ignore symptoms which may have some other cause. Persistent diarrhoea or vomiting, or severe nappy rash, need professional attention regardless of whether the baby is teething at the time.

---

# WHEN CAN YOU EXPECT TEETHING PROBLEMS?

There is a huge range of normal ages for a baby to begin teething. The first tooth can appear before the baby is born, although this is rare (and not ideal if you're breastfeeding).

Generally you can expect to see the first tooth somewhere between three and 12 months, and most commonly around five or six months.

The bottom middle two teeth almost always appear first (not generally at exactly the same time), followed by the top two, and the process then spreads around the mouth outward from this. There are twenty first teeth (or milk teeth) altogether, and they are usually all through by the time the baby is two and a half to three.

If it's any consolation, the pain of teething seems to wear off, or maybe the baby's pain threshhold increases. At any rate, you don't have to go through the teething thing twenty times over two years. Once the first few teeth are through the baby probably won't show any distress about the rest of them.

# HOW WILL YOU KNOW?

The baby may suffer the effects of teething for several weeks before the culprit finally starts to emerge from the gum. So the fact that the baby appears to have no teeth doesn't mean it can't be teething.

Identifying a teething baby isn't always easy even for experienced parents, so it's quite understandable if you're not sure whether the baby is teething or not. The more painful it is, the easier it is to recognise as a rule.

The typical signs of teething are:

- Dribbling

- A very red, flushed cheek on the side the tooth is coming through on, or possibly both cheeks (one normal cheek and one very red one is one of the clearest indications of teething)

- Grumpiness and general 'moaniness'

- Restless or disrupted sleep

- A red and swollen section of gum

- A desire to chew things, assuming the baby is old enough for this to be apparent. It may stick its fingers or fist in its mouth if nothing else is available.

The baby won't necessarily have all these symptoms (that would make it far too easy for you). However, if there are enough of them with no other obvious cause, you can treat the baby for teething and see if it helps. If it does, carry on. If not, don't bother and look elsewhere for the cause if the baby is in sufficient discomfort to warrant it.

# WHAT CAN YOU DO ABOUT IT?

Obviously you want to ease the baby's pain if you can. Scope may be limited, but experiment with any of the following:

- Something to chew on, if the baby is old enough. This could be anything from a teething ring (a ring-shaped toy designed for a baby to chew on) to a piece of raw carrot if the baby is old enough for this – about six months and up. If you can keep something ready in the fridge once you know the baby is teething, the coolness will help it too – whether it's a teething ring or a piece of food.

- A cool drink may also alleviate the discomfort.

- Teething gel. This generally works for half an hour at the most, and many varieties have a maximum dose of once every three or four hours (so check the pack). Some don't, and can be used more frequently, but still shouldn't be overused. Also check for a minimum age; some are only suitable from four months. Teething gel is, in effect, a very mild local anaesthetic gel.

- If the baby is in a lot of discomfort and sleeping badly as a result of the teething, you can give it infant paracetamol solution or ibuprofen.

# Absolute essentials when travelling

## If you bottle feed

Baby

Milk

Bottle
and teat

## If you breastfeed

Baby

Everything else can be
substituted in an emergency

# Travelling with the baby

Nipping out to the shops with the baby in tow is one thing. But going away for the weekend? Or on holiday? What if you forget something essential, how will you cope? Actually, travelling with a baby is arguably easier than travelling with an older child. It may seem daunting the first time or two, but you'll soon get into the swing of it.

**Core objective:** Go away overnight with the baby

**Key focus:** Bring the baby back in one piece

The worry is that you'll forget something essential. But just remember that most of the things you consider essential are unheard of in many non-Western countries, and were only invented relatively recently in evolutionary terms.

What you might think a baby needs, and what a baby actually needs, are a long way apart. So take as much as you like, but don't panic if you forget something.

---

## Myth: travelling with a baby means trekking mountains of baby equipment around with you

You'll probably need to carry a bit more luggage than you used to, but you can still travel relatively light with a baby. It largely depends on you: do you normally travel with a pantechnicon for your own luggage, or just a clean change of underwear and a toothbrush? If you're the minimalist type, you can apply this method – slightly moderated – to travelling with a baby.

---

# WHAT DO YOU NEED?

This is the burning question: what do you have to take with you and what can you leave behind? Well, how long is a piece of string?

You can leave almost everything behind (except the baby – best take that with you), although this might generate extra work making do without. Or you could take everything you might possibly need and have an easy life – and a car you'd be lucky to fit into with all that luggage, or more than the luggage allowance on a plane.

Here's a summary of the main stuff you might want to consider taking if you have a young baby.

## Sleeping stuff

| Could take | Could get by with |
|---|---|
| Moses basket or carrycot or equivalent | A baby that can't yet roll over can sleep anywhere, from a cardboard box to a drawer removed from a chest of drawers. |
| Blankets | If you forget blankets, a towel or your jumper will do fine – or just extra layers of baby clothes (if you remembered them). |
| Pyjamas or sleep suit | I've never understood why babies are supposed to have different clothes at night from in the daytime. For the first few weeks they can't even tell the difference between day and night. |
| Baby monitor | In the absence of a baby monitor, you can always stay close by enough to listen out. |

# Nappy changing stuff

| Could take | Could get by with |
|---|---|
| Changing mat | You don't need a changing mat. Just chuck a towel underneath the baby if you can, or manage on the floor, a bed or a table without one. |
| Cotton wool or wipes | It's a drag being without cotton wool or wipes, but you can improvise with loo paper or even a cloth. It's a bit rough for the baby as a regular routine, but it won't hurt for a change or two until you can acquire something better. |
| Nappies | Being without nappies is a real pain, admittedly. But remember your **key focus:** bring the baby back in one piece. Even an absence of nappies won't prevent you achieving this. Wrap whatever fabric you have to spare round the baby's bum until you can get hold of replacement nappies. |

# Bottle feeding stuff

This, of course, is one area where breastfeeding comes into its own. But if you bottle feed, here are some general pointers.

| Could take | Could get by with |
| --- | --- |
| Steriliser | A steriliser is handy, but bulky to travel with. You could just boil everything for ten minutes and then leave it to cool in the pan of water. |
| Bottles, teats etc | Being without bottles is a problem, I grant you, but unless you're in the back of beyond you should be able to buy a bottle at an all-night chemist. Managing on one bottle is perfectly possible, even though it's a drag doing all that sterilising. |
| Formula milk | OK, you need the formula milk. Don't forget it – put it at the top of your list of 'things to pack'. |
| Scoop | The scoop is normally in the milk tin. If it isn't you could guess the amount for a feed or two until you can get a replacement. I'm not recommending this, mind, but in an emergency it's better than nothing. Remember, too much milk powder might give the baby a stomach upset, while the worst you can do by mixing up the formula too dilute is to leave the baby hungry – in which case it will doubtless let you know. So it's better to underestimate slightly than to overestimate. |
| Sterile water | Sterile water is important, and it should be boiled tap water. Bottled water can contain unsuitable levels of minerals and so on. However, if you're abroad and temporarily have no means of boiling water, you'd be better off using bottled water (not fizzy, obviously, given the choice) for a feed or two until you've organised a kettle, rather than giving the baby unboiled tap water. |

# Washing stuff

| Could take | Could get by with |
|---|---|
| Baby bath | You can bath your baby in a basin, a plastic bowl or – best of all – in your bath with you (best to get someone else to hand the baby to you once you're in, and take it from you before you get out, if you can). Or even (don't tell my mother I said this) don't bath it at all for a few days. |
| Soap and shampoo | Given that you could manage without bathing the baby at all, soap and shampoo have to be a bonus. If you don't have baby soap and shampoo with you, it's better to use just water than adult stuff, especially near the baby's eyes. |
| Baby towel | Any towel will do fine. Or dry the baby off in a spare blanket. If you're holidaying in a warm country you could even let it dry naturally. |

# Transportation stuff

You could take a sling or a pushchair – or both. You can get pushchairs which are more basic than some but fold up conveniently small, so they're less bulky to travel with. Obviously it's possible to transport a baby simply by carrying it, so even a forgotten pushchair or sling is an inconvenience rather than a danger.

# Baby clothes

Modern Western practice dictates that clothes be changed almost daily. However, the baby will come to no harm if it wears the same clothes for a week so long as they aren't wet or soiled – in which case a quick rinse and dry out will sort them out. In fact, no clothes at all is fine if you wrap the baby in blankets or towels instead. I'm not suggesting you're likely to take the baby on holiday stark naked without noticing ('Darling, should this baby be wearing something before we hop on the plane?'). I'm simply illustrating that if you find yourself wishing you'd brought another couple of changes of clothes, it really isn't worth fretting over.

# First aid stuff

My personal view is that the fewer medicines one uses, the better, especially on babies and small children. However, there are times when certain medication can be a big help in easing discomfort. It's a good idea to keep a permanent mini first aid kit ready packed (duplicating medication you use in the house) if you go away at all frequently. Apart from checking the 'use by' dates occasionally, you can just sling the thing in a suitcase and you know you'll have anything you might need. A general 'just in case' first aid kit for a baby could include:

- Cream for nappy rash

- Teething gel

- Infant paracetamol solution for mild fevers/chronic teething etc

That should be enough unless your baby has a specific medical condition.

## Eating stuff

If the baby has started on solid food, you will want to take supplies for it to eat. You'll also have to decide whether or not to take a steriliser (the alternative being boiling everything to sterilise it). Here are a few thoughts:

● Jars of baby food may not be ideal as a permanent diet, but they're fine for a few days. Look for ones with no added sugar or salt.

● You can get plastic cutlery containers (they usually come with baby cutlery inside when you buy them) which you can sterilise. Then you can put a day's supply of sterilised spoons in them to last you until you get back to base.

● Bananas are great when you're travelling. You don't have to sterilise them (in fact I'd like to see you try) and you can break them open and scrape the flesh straight onto the spoon. As handy as a jar of baby food and fresher. You can do the same with avocados.

If you're going somewhere hot and sunny you may want to take some kind of sunshade, as it isn't good for the baby to be out of the shade.

## Make a list

It's a good idea, if this doesn't sound too grown up and over organised, to write down everything you plan to take with you for the baby. You can keep the list for next time, and simply add new items, such as baby foods or favourite toys. If you have a PC you can update the list every time you travel.

# Appendix

## THINGS NOT TO WORRY ABOUT

You'll inevitably worry more than you need with a new baby – you wouldn't be doing your job properly if you didn't.

But there's no point fretting so much it keeps you awake; the baby will do that for you adequately without any help. There are some things that are quite normal in small babies but look really weird. So here's a round-up of some of the main things not to worry about.

Obviously it isn't impossible that some more significant problems could exhibit similar symptoms (not that I'm trying to worry you) so if you're concerned, check with your midwife, health visitor or doctor. However, all of the following have normal and harmless explanations in the vast majority of cases:

## Head moulding

Birth does strange things to the baby's head. It's supposed to. In order to cope with the journey through the birth canal your baby's skull bones are not fully fused together yet. So its head is easily squeezed into a convenient shape for being born. This is not necessarily the head shape you had planned for your baby. It will take a few weeks, or even months, for your baby's head to reshape itself. If your baby is born using forceps or Ventouse (suction) delivery the moulding may be more pronounced.

## Stork marks

A great term for small areas of redness usually on the nape of the neck (hence the name). They are also common on the forehead and eyelids. Probably around half of all babies have them and they do fade with time, though they can take months – or even a year or two – to disappear completely.

## Fontanelles

Another thing not to worry about is your baby's fontanelles. These are soft spots on the head where there is still a gap between the skull bones for several months (usually not fully closed over until about two years old). This is disconcerting because it looks as if there's a hole in the head covered only by skin. You can see the pulse throbbing in this patch too, which somehow adds to the feeling that it's too fragile to cope with. And sometimes, if the baby is really yelling, it can look slightly swollen. However, it's not only entirely normal and proper, but also covered with a thick membrane which makes it much safer than it looks. (If the fontanelle is sunken and the baby isn't feeding, this is a good indicator of dehydration and you should contact your GP.)

## Mongolian blue spot

This is very common in babies of native American, African, Asian or Hispanic descent. There are large blue marks around the base of the spine and the buttocks. They are totally harmless and disappear within a year or so.

## Stray eyelash in the eye

This can look like a line on the surface of the eye. However unless the eye is red or inflamed the best thing is to leave it alone and it will eventually go to the corner of the eye. (I have no idea where all the stray eyelashes – I'm talking adults here too – go after they've reached the corner of your eye.)

## Sudden jumps

Babies often seem to overreact to a sound with a startled jerk. They are also very prone to 'sleep jumps' where they give a sudden jump in their sleep. Both of these are completely normal.

## Vaginal bleeding

Very occasionally, newborn baby girls will have what looks like a light menstrual period, with some bleeding or pinkish mucous loss. It most commonly starts on the fourth day. This has something to do with hormones and is more common in baby girls who are breastfed. It lasts only a few days at most.

## Sticky eyes

These are common before the tear ducts are fully developed. One or both eyes can be watery and collect whitish 'sleep' in the corners. When the baby first wakes, its eyelids may be slightly stuck together. Bathe the eye with cotton wool dipped in warm boiled water, wiping from the nose corner of the eye outwards. If it lasts more than a few days, or turns a yellow or green colour, there may be an infection and you should check with your GP or health visitor.

## Farting

You may need reassuring that a baby's farts are entirely disproportionate to its size; both in volume and frequency.

# Dry skin

This is not uncommon, especially in babies who were born overdue. It's not something to worry about, but keep washing to a minumum (say, one bath a week) and follow it by rubbing in a little olive oil or moisturiser.

# Sweating

Some babies are very sweaty around their heads, and can leave the bedding quite sodden after a sleep. This is perfectly normal. If you're concerned you can always check its temperature.

# Regurgitation

It's entirely natural for babies to bring up some of the milk you took such trouble to get down them. (When you've dragged yourself exhausted from your bed in the middle of the night in response to their cry this can seem like plain bad manners.) However it's just what happens. They often do this as an accompaniment to burping. So long as they are gaining weight steadily and don't appear to be in any discomfort (other than the usual windiness which should ease after they've burped and regurgitated) there's nothing to be concerned about. Some babies are more prone to this than others, and many very healthy babies regurgitate frequently.

If your baby is gaining weight steadily I should stop worrying about the regurgitation and start worrying about where you're going to find time to wash all those clothes you'll be getting through.

## Variation in breathing patterns

It's very typical for a small baby to vary its rate of breathing when it's asleep. As a normal parent you will probably spend far too much time listening intently to every nuance of your baby's breathing. Well, don't worry if it speeds up or slows down. This is what happens when babies sleep. You should consider worrying only if it's accompanied by wheezing, floppiness, a bluish tinge to the skin or other such symptoms.

By the way, it's also normal for babies to pause or break off between sucks when feeding in order to breathe. It doesn't mean they're not feeding properly.

## Milk spots

These are technically known as milia and are raised whitish pimples which appear on the face, neck and sometimes scalp of around forty percent of babies – the areas where a teenager would get acne. They often like to cluster around the bridge of the nose and the cheeks. Milia are caused by the sweat- and oil-secreting glands kicking into action. They can appear anywhere from a week to a month or so after birth, and will go away on their own within a couple of weeks.

## Enlarged breasts

The baby as well you. This is caused by some of the mother's milk-producing hormones leaking through to the baby just before birth. It is equally common in boys and girls and is another thing not to worry about. It usually eases off after a few days, though it can last for months and is still nothing to worry about. In fact, even if the nipples leak a small amount of milky fluid (traditionally known as 'witch's milk') you don't need to fret. Incidentally, one of the more old-fashioned treatments for this was to squeeze the nipples to remove the fluid. This is definitely not recommended so please don't try it at home.

## Red blotches

This benign condition, technically known as erythema toxicum neonatorum, affects between a third and a half of all newborns, almost always within the first four or five days. It's caused by the sweat glands taking time to get into the swing of things. The red blotches can appear almost anywhere, and have raised, clear bumps at the centre. It's very rare in premature babies, and is more likely to occur the higher the birthweight and the longer the gestation. It doesn't bother the baby and will go away by itself, though you can try to speed up the process if you want to by making sure there's good ventilation and the baby isn't overdressed. If the centres of the blotches are yellow and pussy, you're dealing with something else (possibly a secondary infection) and should consult your GP or health visitor.

## Cradle cap

This is a harmless rash that looks like crusty pale yellowy-brown scales on the scalp. If you don't like the look of it and want to try to get rid of it, rub some olive oil into it and leave it for 24 hours. Then comb the baby's hair gently and wash it. You may have to repeat this. Alteratively ignore it and it will go away on its own after a while.

# Hair

It is completely normal for your baby to have lots of hair, no hair at all, or anything in between. It's also normal for most of it to fall out a few weeks after the birth in worryingly large handfuls, usually when you're washing it. It may grow back a very different colour.

# Flattened patch on head

Known as plagiocephaly, it can be alarming to see that the baby has developed a flattened area on its head. However, it's completely harmless and is down to the fact that the baby spends most of its time lying on that part of its head. Once it starts to do things like sitting up, the skull (which is still very flexible) will return to its predestined shape without trouble. I suppose you could pick the baby up more, or keep stimulating it to turn its head, but there's no need to go overboard. You'll upset it more by disturbing its sleep than you will by leaving the thing to sort itself out naturally.

# White threads in pooh

One of the most popular first foods once your baby moves on to solids is mashed banana – and very healthy it is too.

Be prepared, however, for the fact that it can cause small white threads in your baby's pooh which – if you're having a bad day – can look disconcertingly like worms. The acid test is to see if the threads wiggle (honestly, the things you find yourself doing once you're a parent). If not, put it down to the banana and don't worry.

# Try not to worry

If you're at all concerned about your baby the question to ask yourself is, 'Is it a happy, healthy looking baby?' If the answer to this question is yes, and your baby is also feeding well, it is very unlikely that it is suffering from whatever dreadful scenario your over-vivid imagination is dreaming up.

We all worry – if you didn't, you wouldn't be doing your job properly. However, it's no fun fretting, and looking at the bigger picture often helps put your fears into perspective about that-funny shaped toe, or this small red spot, or that excessive farting.

# THINGS TO CONSIDER WORRYING ABOUT

There may be times when you need a doctor to examine and perhaps treat the baby for something more serious than milk spots or funny-coloured pooh. So how can you tell when you need to call in the professionals? There's usually a midwife or health visitor at hand to ask for advice, but here's a guide to the most likely symptoms that should prompt you to call the doctor, and a couple you may be unsure about.

## Vomiting

All babies give you plenty of opportunities to re-examine their food after they've drunk it. For some reason little dribbles and spit-ups of milk are a regular part of having a small baby. You don't need to worry unless the vomiting has one or more of the following characteristics:

● It is projectile

● it is green or yellow (ie bile)

● it is red, especially dark red to brown (ie contains blood)

In addition there are other symptoms you should look for. Get medical help if the baby:

● Is persistently vomiting within half an hour of eating

● Looks yellowish

You should call a doctor urgently, or take the baby to A&E if it also:

● Seems to be in pain

● Has a swollen or tender stomach

● Has had a bump to the head

● Is having breathing problems

● Is dehydrated (sunken eyes, sunken fontanel, cold and mottled hands and feet, extreme sleepiness)

## Choking and breathing difficulties

Frankly choking is pretty rare in the first few months as the baby cannot reach anything to put in its mouth.

Assuming you haven't been giving it buttons to play with or putting marbles in its bed there's not much chance of it choking on such things. However, as your baby gets older accidents can happen, and if you suspect the baby is choking you should call 999. Possible symptoms of this include:

● Coughing

● Dribbling (clearly not a worrying symptom on its own)

● Wheezing

● Breathlessness

- A bluish tinge to the lips, nose and skin

- Inability to breathe

## Temperature and fever

It's normal for a baby's temperature to fluctuate between about 36–38°C (97–100.4°F). You should call a doctor if the baby's temperature rises above:

- 38°C if the baby is under three months old

- 38.3°C if it is three to six months old

- 39.4°C if it is over six months old

There are other symptoms to look out for in this case and mention to the doctor if they occur alongside a raised temperature:

- Change in appetite

- Change in sleeping habits

- Difficulty breathing

- The baby is hot and listless

If the baby has purple blotches or reddish-purple spots which don't disappear when you press a glass against them, call 999 immediately as you need to check for meningitis.

## Pain

Identifying pain in someone who sobs their heart out every time they feel a bit tired may seem near impossible. Babies do have an absurdly low pain threshold – or at least a very low threshold at which they start complaining about pain. However, you get to know your own baby and you'll notice if it yells in a different way or for a different reason or at a different time from usual. It may object to being touched in a particular place. Most commonly this will be the abdomen, but it could be anywhere. Look for any swelling or bruising and give the doctor a call if your baby seems to be in any kind of pain.

## Ear infection

Since they spend most of their time lying down, babies are quite prone to ear infections (forgive the pun).

The tubes in the middle ear spend more time horizontal than vertical and if they get blocked as a result of a cold, for example, bacteria can build up. The doctor can prescribe antibiotics so get in touch if you see the following symptoms:

- Fever

- Diarrhoea

- Fluid leaking from the ears

- The baby pulling at its ear or putting its hand up to it

- Signs of discomfort while eating and swallowing

## Colds

Colds in babies can seem worrying until you get used to them. The good news there is that you should get ample opportunity to get used to them. In fact, babies are very prone to colds until their immune system builds up – as a result of having colds. The average adult gets two to four colds a year, while babies and children can get 10–12 a year.

The more they're exposed to other children, the more colds they're likely to pick up.

If the baby has a cold keep it warm and comfortable. You don't need to call a doctor unless the baby also has:

● A fever that persists

● Diarrhoea

● Vomiting

● Breathing difficulties

It's worth emphasising that while babies do occasionally develop worrying and even serious illnesses, in the overwhelming majority of cases these are resolved without long-term harm to the baby. Take action if you think something may be wrong, and try not to panic.

# BASIC EQUIPMENT

There's a lot of equipment you might want for the baby, and all sorts of gadgets to make your life as a parent easier. But there are only a few real essentials – think how little people have always managed with in the past. So here are two lists. The first gives the absolute minimum you need, and the second lists other items which the baby will survive perfectly happily without but which most parents choose to have. I'm not listing all the myriad things which you could get but which are strictly optional extras (such as bottle warmers, cot monitors which tell you the baby's heart rate, or those things with toys dangling from them that fit across the baby's car seat).

To compensate for all this extra stuff cluttering up your house, there are a few things you can get rid of, since you won't be needing them any more, such as your alarm clock, which is now redundant, and all small or breakable objects less than three feet from the ground.

## Essential stuff

- **Nappies** – plus any thing that goes with the nappies you've chosen, such as nappy pins for terry nappies.

- **Something to clean the baby with.** For when you change its nappy – cotton wool, wipes or something equally soft.

- **Something to bath the baby in.** This might be a bucket or a sink, or a baby bath. You can use a proper bath but unless you're in it with the baby it can be too big and slippery to begin with.

- **Some kind of soap.** Preferably one formulated for babies or one with no chemicals, perfumes or colours in it that may irritate the baby's skin.

- **A towel.** In fact, two is even better. They don't need to be baby towels.

- **Something for the baby to sleep in.** A crib, carrycot or Moses basket are the usual choices.

- **A mattress.** The advice here is not to use a second-hand mattress as this can increase the risk of SIDS (cot death).

- **Bedding.** Don't use pillows or quilts until the baby is 12 months because there's a risk of suffocation. Use sheets and several light blankets rather than one thick one.

- **A car seat of some kind** – assuming the baby will ever travel in a car. It is illegal to hold the baby in your arms in the front of the car, and only legal in the back if there is no seat belt in the car. Even then, it's extremely dangerous, and I would strongly advise that you don't do it. If you don't have some kind of car seat, this could make getting home from the hospital pretty tricky, unless you live within walking distance. The choice of car seats is daunting, but any good shop assistant will talk you through it. The main thing to appreciate is that you will have to upgrade at some point, since there is no car seat which fits the baby from birth until it's old enough to sit on the seat properly like everyone else.

- **If you're bottle feeding you'll need** bottles with teats and caps, and sterilising equipment (which can simply be a large pan to boil water in).

- **If you're bottle feeding you'll also need** formula milk (tinned, powdered baby milk).

- **Clothes.** It's far easier to control the baby's temperature if you dress it in layers of thin clothes which you can remove as and when you need to. Make sure anything in contact with its skin is soft. Natural fabrics are preferable.

Babies don't worry too much about fashion, but they do like to be comfortable (maybe they're practising for old age).

## Useful but not essential stuff

- **Changing mat.** To change the baby's nappy on.

- **Changing bag.** To hold all the nappy changing stuff when you're out. A carrier bag does fine, though you can buy fancy bags and rucksacks with lots of pockets and zips.

- **Some means of carrying the baby.** This can be a sling, pushchair or pram. There's a terrifying array of these to choose from, including car seats which adapt into a pram or pushchair, pushchairs which lie the baby right back horizontally to sleep, carrycots on wheels and many more.

  Ask other parents for advice, and shop assistants, and then make the best guess you can as to what you'll want. It's often worth having both a sling and something on wheels.

- **If you're breastfeeding, you'll probably want** nursing bras (which open at the front) to make things easier.

- **Bibs.**

- **Clean-up cloths.** For clearing up everything from milk to... well, never mind what, just make sure you have plenty of cloths. You can buy muslin squares cheaply from baby shops, or you can just cut up old T-shirts or anything else absorbent.

# A final word...

The important thing to bear in mind when the baby arrives is not to take things too seriously. The first few weeks can be tough in many ways, but do try to have as much fun as you can too. Bringing up a baby successfully isn't rocket science; even really dumb animals like sheep and chickens manage it (and they don't come much dumber than that) so you can certainly do it.

Just stay focused on the essentials, and don't sweat the details. If the baby isn't crying, it's happy. That should be good enough for anyone. If it is crying, it probably only needs some milk or a bit of a nap, or maybe a warm blanket over it. It's very simple really. Throw in the odd nappy change, bath the thing occasionally, and that's it really.

A warm, dry, well-fed baby will get so much more benefit and enjoyment from being with a happy parent than it will from having a change of vest or the latest designer buggy. So don't get distracted by all the clutter and everyone else's advice. Don't waste time ironing baby clothes, or scouring the shops for a state-of-the-art steriliser, or fretting about how many boxes of nappies to take on your weekend away.

All that matters is a happy, healthy baby with parents who have time to enjoy it. Put all your efforts into the baby, yourself and each other, and let everything else wait.

Good luck and have fun.